ACCEPTED!

GETTING IN AND FITTING IN AT
HARVARD BUSINESS SCHOOL

*An International Student Reporting
on Life at HBS*

FREDERIC D MAHIEU

Disclaimer:

The opinions expressed in this book are the author's. This book is not endorsed, sponsored or authorized by Harvard Business School or any of its affiliates, nor by any of the other companies, organizations, people or products mentioned in this writing. Every effort has been made to represent events in the most truthful and correct way. Should there be any concerns with regards to the truthfulness of events mentioned, please contact the author.

The author is not an expert on the HBS admission process and cannot be held responsible for how following his advice in this book impacts a school applicant's admission outcome.

The events are portrayed to the best of the author's memory. While all the stories in this book are true, some names and identifying details have been changed to protect the privacy of the people involved.

ISBN 978-981-09-9168-5
eISBN 978-981-09-9169-2

Book design by Victoria Valentine / www.pageandcoverdesign.com

"It was the best of times..."

"It was the worst of times..."

It was my time at HBS

The times described in this book

IV. What happens outside the classroom, stays outside the classroom

V. Giving HBS a bad name

VI. The remarkable HBS assets

ACCEPTED!
GETTING IN AND FITTING IN AT
HARVARD BUSINESS SCHOOL

Introduction

Meet Simon – Harvard undergrad, GPA[1] of 3.8, and 4 years of experience in investment banking. Dreamed of going to Harvard Business School (HBS) from birth.

Meet Elaine – fun, outgoing personality. Mom went to HBS. Dad went to HBS. Actually, her parents met at HBS. Works at her parents' company. Strong interpersonal skills and a rich extra-curricular resume to boot.

And then there's … Me! – a bit shy and rather introverted. Son of a pastry chef. An ok academic record. Regular corporate job. Stands out in small groups but prefers to hide in bigger crowds.

When one thinks about a typical HBS student, people would imagine a Simon or an Elaine kind of person. Effective, social, type-A[2] personalities. And for most of them, HBS is a clear milestone on their path to professional success – it is the place and time in their lives where they build their networks and skills for the future. For me, things were a bit different. Of course I knew about Harvard and HBS from a young age – who doesn't? But I hadn't been planning to go to school there since I was 16. Rather, it was a set of personal and professional circumstances that led me there quite unexpectedly.

Similarly, this book was not something I planned for either. After getting into HBS (and going through the painstaking process of writing the application essays) I decided that I really needed to improve my writing skills. Prior to applying to HBS, I struggled to find value-adding information about the school written by actual students. I thought that a blog on my experiences at HBS would fill this "market gap". It would be useful to others considering applying, and it seemed to make sense as a way to keep myself motivated to write as a means of improving my writing skills.

Over time, I watched my blog readership grow way beyond what I expected. People told me they liked the quirkiness of my writing and the honesty I used in describing my experiences at HBS.

---

1   GPA = Grade Point Average. It is a number that represents the average of grades received over all courses. Highest GPA is 4.0.
2   Type A personality is a reference to the Type A and Type B personality theory developed by the cardiologists Meyer Friedman and Ray Rosenman. Type As are excessively competitive, ambitious, driven, and often known to be workaholics.

Moreover, I believe that my international view (I was a real international student with no experience in the U.S. prior to HBS – more on that later) also helped people not so familiar with the U.S. or HBS to gain a better understanding of life there. I wanted to address all of these aspects in my blog. The blog eventually led to this book.

This book might be unlike other books that you'll read on HBS. This is because it is not your typical "How to get in" book. It is not a book aimed at hyping the whole experience either. It was written by someone I consider to be a bit different from the average HBS crowd – me. And finally, it will have an international/European view on a very American experience.

I organized my thoughts in more than a hundred short chapters. The book can be read from beginning to end, or one can just page through it to read topics that look interesting or relevant. I start off talking about my road to HBS – how I got in and what it took me to get my application in on time – and discuss all kinds of other experiences, including everything from the classroom seating chart to HBS dating etiquette. While reading this book, you might notice that I am someone who loves observing things, situations and people. This is reflected throughout the book, as I will be focusing from time to time on some details others might not have noticed.

I hope this book will be a fun read both for HBS alums, current HBS students and of course, those who are thinking of applying to HBS. But even if you have no intention whatsoever to apply to business school, this book might just be a relaxing read to satisfy your curiosity about HBS. Or, who knows, maybe you'll be able to fool your friends into believing you are an actual HBS grad – with data and a lot of unique stories from this book to reinforce that!

Enjoy the read!

Find an overview of all referenced online materials in this book as well as additional information at the following link: **http://goo.gl/KRupzu**

PART

I

THE ROAD TO HBS

1

My personal road to HBS

I must have only been a teenager when I associated the Harvard brand with distinctive features such as 'quality education,' 'best school in the world,' and 'totally unattainable.' But beyond this I knew very little about the HBS environment.

I grew up in Europe, about 3,500 miles away from the Harvard campuses in Boston and Cambridge, MA[3]. Harvard didn't have fancy TV commercials in my country telling me what it was about. I didn't have any friends or family that were alumni or that were related in any way to Harvard (or to the U.S. for that matter).

In fact, my Dad was a pastry chef, and together with my Mom, they started and ran a successful local pastry business in Brussels, Belgium. I was the first one in my family to go to college and barely had to pay any fees for it in the highly subsidized educational space in Belgium. I grew up in a protected environment, which left me a bit naïve until a later age about how the world, and more specifically the business world, worked.

My knowledge of the English language was average before reaching 18, when I spent one summer living and working in a hotel/restaurant in Bournemouth, UK. My English improved dramatically through that experience (as did my table waiting skills), but I'm learning new things even now and I still struggle to pronounce that bloody English 'r' in the 'wight' way, making even my name (which contains two of them) a hard job to pronounce[4].

I graduated from college with a degree in Economics and Business. On a professional level, I had about seven years of experience – a lot more than most HBS students – working for a multinational company. I had worked in a set of different roles, from finance to strategic supply chain functions, and had been promoted on several occasions.

---

3   MA is short for Massachusetts – it is the state in the U.S. where the school is located. All states in the U.S. have their own two letter abbreviation.
4   My struggles with the 'r' even led me to use the name 'James' when ordering drinks at Starbucks to avoid having to repeat my real name on several occasions to the baristas.

However, it wasn't as if my background had "Harvard material" written all over it. Truth be told, it was life and its many mysterious ways that led me to successfully apply to HBS. It was partially linked to my love for an American woman (and her continued attempts to get me to move to the U.S.). Going to business school was a way for me to move across "the pond"/the Atlantic Ocean without having to deal with difficult visa issues. It was also linked to my untamable curiosity for things – a curiosity that peaked when I visited Boston and sat in on a class at HBS prior to applying[5].

Ultimately, I consider myself an HBS outcast – someone who got in by mistake, through the stubbornness of my American girlfriend and by a mysterious drive and aptitude that would take ahold of me in times that I really wanted to get something.

It's the combination of those things – Harvard's amazing marketing of its brand and some interesting games of fate – that got me to experience the renowned two year Harvard Business School MBA program.

The experience was a unique one that I shared with others through my blog – HBSTimes.com. And I now want to share this experience with many others through this writing. And maybe, just maybe, this book may play a role in others' twists of fate. Maybe even yours for that matter…

2

Prerequisites to getting into Harvard Business school…

A lot of what is good and interesting in life tends to be scarce – and so is the number of available seats at the top business schools. HBS accepts about 900 new students each year. With an acceptance rate of around 10% of applicants, receiving an acceptance letter from HBS is the result of a very competitive process. The whole process to completing an application for HBS is well documented and can be found on the HBS website. There is

---

5   More on that in later chapters – but highly recommended for those wanting to apply to HBS!

also a whole industry focused on offering services to prospective students to help them prepare the best application possible.

Overall, there are six major roadblocks on your way to business school: two standardized tests (the TOEFL for testing your English skills[6], and the GMAT to test you on math, language and "miauw"[7]), an application including three letters of recommendation and a couple of essays[8], and finally an interview with HBS staff. Other business schools often rely on alumni to conduct interviews at international locations, but all HBS interviews are done by members of the MBA admissions board.

Each of these roadblocks has a specific goal in the application. What is important here is to understand these roadblocks from HBS's point of view – what do they want, and why? Understanding that is an important element of getting through them. In the following table, you'll find an overview of the requirements of the HBS application. In the next chapters, I will dive into my personal experience with different parts of the application.

---

6   Only applicable for international students.
7   The Miauw will be explained in the following chapter.
8   Please note that the process described here is the one I went through for my application to the class of 2014. Admission procedures change on a yearly basis and are documented on the HBS website. The admissions process for the class of 2015 no longer included mandatory essays.

The roadblocks	What people think HBS is looking for	What you might want to get across
TOEFL score (international students only)	Good knowledge of English	Good knowledge of English
GMAT score	Intelligence	Motivation to get into a top business school – GMAT is mostly about studying, not being intelligent
Overall application / CV	Was I doing interesting and/or relevant things?	Have you demonstrated the potential to (continue to) stand out in the future?
Letters of recommendation from previous bosses and/or colleagues	How well did I do in my previous job?	Do you have a good network? How well are you able to network?
Essays on several subjects	Can I organize my ideas in a good way? Can I write?	What about my background makes me stand out? What potential do I have to do great things? How will I represent HBS going forward?
Interviews	Do I know my job? Can I explain my CV further?	Can I stand up for myself? Can I engage with others?

The process is long and hard, and can be very frustrating at times (especially in the last couple of days before the deadline!). I personally spent a lot of time studying for my GMAT and underestimated the amount of time to spend on essays. Moreover, to be on the safe side, most students combine applying at different schools at the same time, increasing stress and workload for the different steps mentioned above. And for those who think they can 'copy-paste' essays from one school application to the other – forget it. Every essay for every application requires special attention.

Preparation is key – knowing what HBS is looking for is even more important. My best advice here is: know exactly what story you want to tell HBS (and other schools). Your whole application should be focused on a message you want to reinforce through your resume, your essays and even your letters of recommendation.

Find more info on all of these application steps in the following sections. I hope that they provide some important guidance on the overall process to successfully apply to HBS.

3

The G-what? The GMAT? Or the G-CAT?!

The GMAT (Graduate Management Admissions Test) is a standardized test used specifically for admission into graduate level business programs. It is hence a required test for the application process to HBS[9]. A lot of people consider the GMAT to be an intelligence test – that is just a rumor spread by those with high GMAT scores. In reality, the GMAT is closer to testing a student's level of dedication and discipline to the test. Sure, a basic level of intelligence is required – as is having some fluency with numbers. I am convinced though that one is not born with the skills to do well on the GMAT, but that one learns how to take this test successfully. It is all about spending the right amount of time and energy.

The type of questions found on the GMAT often require the test-taker to know which framework to use to answer a question. As an example, let's start off by looking at a typical GMAT question:

The total number of black cats is 25% greater than the number of black male cats, and the number of all female cats is 5 times the number of black female cats. If the male cats are 50% of all cats, then what percent of male cats are black? Choose between the following answers: 10, 20, 40, 50, 80[10].

Got it? Great! Just to make sure, double-check your answer with the

9   Some other standardized tests are also accepted at most business schools, such as the GRE (Graduate Record Examination).
10   As seen on MasterTheGMAT, now GMAT Tutor: **http://goo.gl/jKbbY2**

solution provided at the end of this chapter. What framework did you use to come to that answer? Or did you just know how to calculate this based on prior knowledge?

The origin of the GMAT dates back to the early fifties. Questions relating to black cats have been administered for more than 60 years! It began with only nine business schools (including Wharton, Kellogg, Booth, Columbia and HBS) discussing the possibility of defining a standardized entry test for their graduate programs. In 1954, the first tests were taken. It took only 25 years (in 1981) before 200,000 tests would be conducted on an annual basis – an amazing number considering that only U.S. based schools used the GMAT up until 1995. In recent years, 250,000 take the GMAT annually.

A good GMAT score does not guarantee an entry ticket to HBS – but it sure helps. 50% of the HBS MBA class of 2014 had a GMAT of 730[11] or more (out of a maximum of 800), i.e. the 96th percentile and above. With 90% of successful applicants having scores of 670 (or 85th percentile) or more, any score below 670 might dramatically reduce your chances of making it into HBS.

So how did I do? Well, I studied for the GMAT for about two months. This meant reading up on theory during weekdays after long days at work and doing practice GMAT tests over the weekends. Theory reviews are long and painful, and require diving into some basic math and grammar rules. Remember the Pythagoras theorem? And how to measure the diameter of a circle? To be more effective during the test, it is also important to remember the basic rules of multiplication, as calculators are not allowed during the test. It may seem a little silly, but I actually reviewed my multiplication tables.

I found the practice tests to be very important. I set aside about five hours for a full practice GMAT exam – this would include the time of taking the test and, more importantly so, the time to review my answers and to understand where I went wrong. I did one test a week for the first couple of weeks, then one test on Saturday and one on Sunday in the five weeks prior to the exam.

---

11 The average score on the GMAT of HBS applicants has been steadily increasing over the years, with the average score evolving towards 750 nowadays.

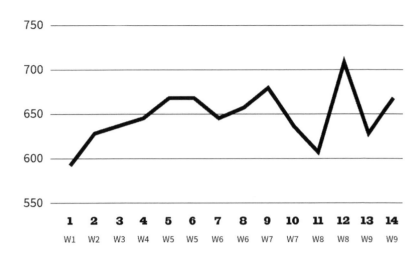

My practice exam test scores... all 14 of them...

I completed about 14 full-scale test exams in the nine weeks leading up to the exam. Only once did I manage to beat the 700-point barrier – a target I had set for myself. In the first couple of weeks, I had seen a gradual improvement in my test score results. Then in week 8, disaster struck in the form of a very low score of 610. The next day, I had my all-time high with 710! But in the end, none of those scores were of importance – only my performance on the final exam would matter.

I still have a vivid memory of the whole GMAT test-taking experience. First, I had to register online with GMAC[12]. There are GMAT test centers all over the world – there are even on-base test centers for the military community. For most people, accessibility should not be a problem. After registering for the test in my preferred location, I had to decide on a date. As I was aiming for late August (just a couple of weeks before the first-round application deadlines of most business schools), I knew I wouldn't have much room for error. I wouldn't have time to retake the test before round 1 application deadlines at the top business schools. However, I decided to take more time to prepare for the test than to take multiple tests half prepared.

---

12 Find a link to GMAC's website here: **http://goo.gl/LTtk7O**

And then there was test day. The test was held in a small office in downtown Brussels, Belgium. After some thorough identity checks, I was guided into a room with just two computers. The computer on the right had a young woman working on it. The other one would be mine. For the next 3-4 hours, it would just be me with the computer… or not? As I had a camera continuously pointing at me throughout the test (to check up on cheaters?), I didn't feel quite as lonely during the test as I expected…

The test started off with the essay-writing part – not something I had spent a lot of time practicing for and not something that is considered in the aggregate GMAT score. The essay score is reflected separately on the GMAT results sheet and would only be communicated weeks after the test itself, unlike the GMAT score which you receive straight after the test[13]. Once the essays were out of the way, I started digging into a labyrinth of math and grammar questions.

What I will never forget is that at the end of the test, I felt really bad about my performance. I didn't have time to answer all of the questions – and I had found some of them extremely harsh and difficult. Once my time was up, the computer gave me the chance to 'cancel' my test results, before knowing how I did. I believe this feature is built in as an option for people who are unwell during the test to avoid a bad test score on their record – but let me tell you that this option can mess with your mind! I hesitated for a moment, thinking about cancelling my results, but decided not to in the end. It was minutes later, when I walked out of the test room that I realized I had almost done something really stupid. Here I was with a 730 GMAT score – the median score of HBS grads. The guy running the test center told me he hadn't seen this kind of result for a couple of years under his watch. This was the moment where I knew – game on, HBS!

Some final pointers for test takers:
- Don't waste too much time and energy in preparing for the essay-writing part of the exam – business schools don't seem to care about your

---

13 I only scored on the 20th percentile for the essay writing part of the exam. Not something to brag about. Not being a native English speaker might make HBS more forgiving for that part of the test.

performance on that part and the result is not part of your final GMAT score. Again, just my personal opinion

- Get help! And go the digital way – forget about books and other outdated tools. I used websites that guided me through all kinds of theory and exercises, and they have the added benefit of repeating more questions on the items that you tend to perform poorly on. Most of them provide excellent practice tests as well. I used MasterGMAT.com[14] at the time (meanwhile acquired by The Economist – how about that for a measure of quality!), but there are tons of other resources out there. MasterG-MAT.com is not cheap, but worth the investment
- My best piece of Belgian advice – eat a piece of chocolate before the test – it did wonders for me
- Never ever stop working on a practice question before fully understanding the dynamics of how to answer it
- Create a sheet with the key rules and theorems used in the GMAT
- Don't ever panic during the test. The GMAT questions you will get are a result of your performance on PREVIOUS questions during the test. If you answer a lot of questions correctly, the following questions will become increasingly difficult, allowing you to dramatically improve your score. So the more you struggle with the questions, the better you might actually be doing during the test! Don't let the GMAT mess with your mind over that

Finally, before giving you the answer to the black cat mystery, find some interesting facts on the GMAT below[15]:

- In 2011, 45% of GMAT exams were taken in the U.S. (down from 53% just four years earlier)
- 77% of examinees of the GMAT would attend a U.S.-based school in 2011 (down from 83% in 2007)
- 40% of GMAT tests are taken by women. However, in China, more women than men take the GMAT

---

 14 MasterGMAT.com is now part of The Economist. Find them here: **http://goo.gl/jKbbY2**
15 Source: GMAC website **http://goo.gl/LTtk7O**

- Men tend to slightly outperform women on the test, with the median score for men totaling 554 compared to 530 for females (except in East and Southeast Asia, where they score the same).
- The highest median score can be found in the 'Australia and Pacific islands' region.

As promised, find the result to the black cat mystery below. Miauw![16]

Any cat can be either male or female, and black or not black. Take x as the number of black male cats. With the information provided, and assuming that there are 100 male cats, you can build the following table:

	Black	Other	Total
Male	x	100-X	100
Female	20	80	100
Total	1.25x	180-X	200

Now we can write the following equation: x+20=1.25x
Which we can simplify to: 20=0.25x
Or, finally: x=80

4

The HBS essays – be more than just a GMAT number!

Studying for the GMAT and writing the HBS essays defines the major part of the workload related to an HBS application. Because the GMAT is a standardized test, the essays are your opportunity to differentiate yourself from all the other applicants in a non-standardized way.

For my application, I wrote four essays in response to the following questions asked by HBS. The first one, "Tell us about three of your accomplishments," (600 words limit) was the easiest one to write. We all have

---

16 Black cat language for 'Good luck!'

some success stories, right? It is a great opportunity to brag about yourself, which really is the goal of this essay. The second essay is similar in nature – "Tell us three setbacks you have faced," also with a 600 word limit. The challenge here is to come up with a couple of setbacks that do not make you look like a total screw-up. Number 3 and 4 were much more challenging for me – "Why do you want an MBA?" (400 words) and "Answer a question you wish we'd asked" (400 words). For the latter question, I chose to ask myself the following: "Describe a time when you had to make a difficult decision"[17].

Recently, HBS has changed its policy towards the essays. They are no longer mandatory. In fact, applicants can just send in an essay on whatever topic they want[18]. I am not sure if the key reason for doing so is linked to the loss of confidence in the authenticity of the essays (all kinds of businesses offer essay-writing and essay-editing services nowadays, making the question of whether or not students actually write the essays themselves a valid one) or if the reason is a more strategic one. Whatever the underlying motivations, HBS tends to have its application policies evolve continuously – and I am sure they have a clear strategy as to why they do so.

Whether you write your essays with the help of an editing service or not, at the end of the day, what really matters is that you stand out amidst thousands of other candidates who are often at least as qualified – if not more – than you are. You have to come with a unique story. You need to portray yourself as someone who has done challenging things in life, whether being an investment banker, being in the military, or working for a non-profit. But it doesn't even have to be anything like that – it could be how you were leading the local football team, the disciplined way in which you taught yourself how to play the guitar or the project which you did that led to great benefits. It's about identifying and discussing the things you've done in life that have made an impact.

Personally, I found writing the essays the most taxing bit of the application process. The whole exercise can become very emotional, and not

---

17 Find my 'winning' essays at the end of this book.
18 Keep in mind that these things keep on evolving on a continuous basis – I describe the situation as it was when I applied to HBS to join the Class of 2014.

only because of a lack of sleep by having to write them for nights in a row. It required a lot of self-reflection and effort. It caused me pain and joy. It made me feel confused and excited. One essay even led to teary eyes while proofreading it to my girlfriend. As such, I strongly encourage you to use the essay-writing part of the application to reflect on what is important to you in life and if business school is indeed what you want/need going forward. This is probably the hardest part for most of us.

Realize, however, that the stories you pen down in essays for HBS don't need to be about building a hospital in the developing world or about closing a financial deal worth millions of dollars. I have had a very normal life, with a normal corporate career. What HBS is looking for is not necessarily what you have done, but what you might end up doing! HBS wants to understand who you are as a person and see if you have the potential to excel in your life going forward. They want to know how you reacted in different situations you confronted in life. They are looking for your aspirations, not just your achievements to date. As such, make sure the essays encompass your strengths, your career, and your views on the future. Think carefully about which stories you want to share. Ideally, use stories that feel the most real to you. I think the most effective essay I wrote was the one that made me feel emotional when writing it.

5

On Sale – Me, myself, my CV, my recommendations and I

With your GMAT scores and your HBS essays in the bag, you can start working your way through the rest of the application process. HBS uses the same online application tool used by Stanford, Wharton and MIT. While the interface is the same for all schools, the types of questions asked are different so it is impossible to copy information from one application tool to another.

The online form will require you to list typical information such as your name and address, but quickly focuses on more detailed aspects of your life. There are questions on your nationality and race. You are questioned on any family ties with the school you might have (has anyone in your family attended HBS?). And finally, sharing your work experience goes beyond your achievements – the school wants insight on your salary for all the jobs you held.

Your professional experience is key to HBS – not so much what you did is important; rather, the school will focus on how you did it. While most of the application is about you selling yourself to HBS, when it comes to your professional experience, you need three other people to sell you as well. Letters of recommendation are very common in the U.S., but not so in most of continental Europe. I was lucky enough to have worked for some amazing people who are not only great professionals and managers, but also great coaches and – as it turned out – excellent writers of letters of recommendation.

While HBS allows the people you have assigned as your recommenders to send in the letters through an online link sent to them, all three of them sent me their letters for review first. While I didn't feel the need to edit them, I was overjoyed reading their letters and the praise they contained. It was also great that these people, often on a very busy schedule, took the time to reflect on me as a person and as a professional, and to write these views down. My only advice? – make sure you have some people you respect that you keep close to in whatever organization you work for. They will be key players in your application process. Tell them about your application strategy and the key message you want to convey in your application – this will help them focus on the right topics and further build on your story[19].

Besides your professional experience, HBS cares a lot about your academic performance as well. Interestingly so, this was more tricky for me to disclose than one would expect. Growing up in continental Europe, I had never been rated based on A's or B's in my life. I didn't even know what GPA[20] stood for. My courses had always been rated as a number out of 20

---

19 I heard from other students however that they would intentionally spread different qualities amongst their 3 recommendations, as such having each recommender specify different characteristics of the student. Seems like a winning strategy as well.

20 GPA = Grade Point Average. It is a number that represents the average of grades received over all courses. Highest GPA is 4.0.

– say 14/20. Full year results would then be averaged out vs 100%[21] (taking into account the weight of the different classes). As such, my full-year score would look something like 70%. On top of that, scores in Europe are not comparable to what they are in the U.S. The U.S. educational system has long suffered from a process of grade inflation, where a lot of students get very high grades. Compare this to my college in Belgium where scores of 70% were considered high. Anything close to 80% was considered brilliant (and very rare for that matter). So I did worry when telling HBS about my passing grades of between 70 and 75% for my academic career. But on the other hand, I think they know that Europe has more of a grade deflationary trend compared to what is happening in the U.S. (find out more about grading in later chapters).

Then there's the resume part of the application. Most applicants already have their resume ready-made. However, for international students, be aware of some of the specificities of U.S. and HBS resumes. First of all, do not divulge any personal information such as your age or race (or a photo for that matter that could divulge that information). This isn't standard to include on resumes in the U.S. and that information will be available on other parts of your application anyway. Second, keep it short and well organized – stick to one page only! Third, focus very much so on what you achieved (e.g. $1 million cost saving by doing xxx) compared to what you did (I was managing a cost savings project). Also, throw in some fancy titles in the process if possible – but don't lie! HBS has a company working for them that will actually contact the company/companies you worked for to check on the accuracy of your working title and responsibilities. But then again, lying is never a good idea, is it? HBS people don't lie![22]

A final aspect of your application is one you have little or no control over. HBS is constantly looking for diversity (nationality / gender / race / educational and professional background) amongst its student body[23]. For example, as a Caucasian U.S. male, the competition to get into HBS might be extremely tough (due to the high number of applicants from that cat-

---

21 Turns out there are websites that allow you to converge your % scores into a GPA – I used **http://goo.gl/deh4N8**

22 Yes, there's a chapter on ethics later in the book.

23 And yes again, more on that later as well.

egory). Not much one can do about this here – my only recommendation would be to apply using the most exotic passport you might have (should you have more than one). Holding a Belgian passport definitely played to my advantage when applying – there are only 10 million of us in the world!

Finished sending in your application? Now sit and wait and hope to be invited for the next milestone in the application process – the HBS interview!

6

The HBS interview – four eyes see more than just two

A couple of months after I completed my HBS application, I got great news from Boston: I was selected for an interview! I was delighted and immediately started looking into the date and venues offered by HBS to conduct the interview. The dates are allocated on a first come, first serve basis, so some healthy haste is advised. While HBS offers a lot of (international) locations for the interview, I decided to fly from Europe to Boston to do mine (I wanted to go there to see my American girlfriend anyway). It's a great opportunity to visit the campus and be part of a class session if you haven't (I had).

I vividly remember walking into the waiting room for the interview. I was surrounded by hyper nervous kids (some of them looked really young). I tried to start a conversation with the guy sitting next to me. He looked young, and his voice couldn't hide how nervous he was. I learned he was in the Army. He had served in Iraq and now wanted to pursue a career in business – HBS would be his launching platform to do so. So here's this kid who probably experienced some of the most horrible things while serving in a war almost losing it over an interview with the HBS admissions team.

Once I got called in for the interview itself, two things stood out to me. First, there are two (not just one) people conducting the interview[24]. One person asks the questions; the other is introduced as 'the observer.' The latter just sat there, literally 'observing' me. I don't think I even heard the sound of his voice at any point during the conversation. I don't even think

---

24   This only seems to be the case for on-campus interviews though.

he said 'hi'. This situation made me feel a bit uncomfortable. Who was I supposed to look at while speaking? But then again, maybe that's the point of having that guy there – to read your body language and see how you respond to uncomfortable situations.

Second, during my interview, I was surprised that the lady interviewing me kept asking questions on the same topic over and over again. She had picked one line on my resume and continually asked questions about that one project I worked on. She didn't let go, tried to corner me with tricky questions, and waited to see how I would defend my work against her acted lack of respect for the work done. I stayed calm, reinforced my message by giving clear examples about how I dealt with the challenges I faced on the project[25]. Most of all, I tried to stay as natural as possible and responded to her queries as I would in everyday life to a colleague, instead of being on the receiving end of an interview.

Overall, I rather enjoyed my interview. I was myself. That even meant I threw in the occasional little joke once in a while, making both the interviewer and her stoic observer friend laugh. It was a risky move, but it paid off!

Final advice: be natural – be yourself. Do a lot of mock interviews up front and prepare for typical resume and personal life questions. Memorize the first line of all of the answers you prepared, so you are sure to start off on the right foot and in the right direction – that is key! Then practice practice practice! And my final Belgian tip is – have some chocolate prior to going in! It did the trick for me!

---

25 It seems that for students with a more technical background, the HBS interviewers prefer to ask questions on specific models and concepts. A student with a background in banking or trading for example might be asked about the specifics of financial derivatives they dealt with. A possible reason for this could be the case-based approach at HBS, where students sometimes need to act as a teacher to the rest of the class lacking knowledge in a particular topic.

7

The acceptance letter and the change in power balance – now YOU are in control

HBS informs students when they can expect an answer on the outcome of their application. I had noted the exact date and time in my agenda, but had told nobody about it, not even my girlfriend at the time. When that moment arrived, I wanted to have some time for myself to absorb it – whether the result was positive or negative.

So there I was, on December 19, 2011, at 6PM local time, sitting in front of my computer and duly pressing the 'SEND/RECEIVE' button on my email application. I will never forget that the email came two minutes late (damn you HBS), but all was forgiven when the message finally loaded into my inbox and I discovered the good news. I had been admitted to HBS! And while I had been admitted to other schools in the weeks and days prior to December 19th, this was the only result that really mattered for me. HBS had been my number 1 choice since I began the application process.

For a moment there, I felt like Tom Cruise in Mission Impossible. I had achieved a difficult goal I had given myself – one that was not written in the stars for me. And it was good being alone when I got the news. It allowed me to fully absorb it and treat myself with a good old slap on the shoulder.

Only five minutes later, my continental-European-self brought me back to earth, and it struck me what this actually meant going forward. About 7 to 8 months from that moment, I would quit my job, move to the U.S. for two years and leave family and friends behind.

I had lived abroad before (one year in Spain, 3 months in the UK and then some shorter stints elsewhere) and had traveled extensively (thanks to the generous Belgian holiday allocation), but only now did I realize the life-changing impact of going to HBS, and just from a practicalities point of view! But almost simultaneously I decided I had to do it – and not doing it would probably leave me regretting it for the rest of my life. So I had a piece of chocolate and told myself – game on HBS! Here I come!

Now I was ready for the fun part – devising strategies on how to inform girlfriend/family/friends of the news. After the announcements and some small celebrations, the time came to kindly say 'Thanks, but no thanks' to some other schools I applied to. Then I started going on a well-deserved power trip on HBS. Yes – a power trip. Just think about it, since the beginning of the application process, HBS was in charge of everything. They could make me do anything, from standardized tests on black cats to begging for recommendation letters among (former) bosses. And I haven't even mentioned all the hours spent on completing the online application tool, where they want to know every little thing about you, your life, up to every salary ever earned. And then there was the interview grill!

Then overnight, the roles changed. Now, HBS needs you to want them! Business schools are obsessed by their rankings, and one of the statistics used in most of these rankings is the % of admitted students that accept the offer of the school (also known as the "yield"). In the case of HBS, this number is well above 90% – and they have every incentive to keep it high![26]

So look who's in charge now – indeed, now it's my turn to be convinced by them to accept their offer. First, playtime! Enjoy the gifts they send you (I got a nice case to carry papers), have them reach out to you multiple times to convince you of choosing the 'right' business school and overload them with practical questions. Second, paytime. Dominate the conversations with HBS on financial aid. #PowerTrip!

---

26 In most cases, students will clearly prefer school A over B when accepted to both. This creates an interesting dilemma in some instances. Imagine someone is accepted at two schools of equal standing – HBS and Stanford Graduate School of Business (on most MBA rankings, these schools rank #1 and #2). In this case, one of these top schools will lose out on their acceptance yield statistic. One could think that both HBS and Stanford thus would benefit from making a deal between them and exchange information on students that have applied to both schools, in order to only accept them at one of both. While I am sure that both schools will deny the existence of this kind of deal, some evidence can be found in the fact that both HBS and Stanford have been 'specializing' in some kind of specific profiles, with HBS focusing on more classical business profiles, and Stanford going more after creative or scientific backgrounds. But this is only a thought that came into existence in my brain – and I have no scientific evidence to prove any of it! And yes, choosing between Harvard and Stanford would be a tough one anyways.

While HBS offers financing[27], there are a lot of other sources of funding that can be found. Some get the corporate deal, in which a company or institution will sponsor the HBS tuition fee. Other companies even continue to pay an employees' salary while at HBS![28] Other people obtain financial support from institutions such as Fulbright. Personally, I combined a limited amount of corporate funding with a grant that got me a $100,000 loan that is interest-free – but to be repaid within five years of graduation[29].

Once you get the funding all sorted out, wait until the last couple of days before the deadline and then just say yes to HBS. HBS, here I come!

8

More work at the horizon – the start of the HBS checklists...

So you got your acceptance letter, the finances are all sorted out, you told HBS you're coming, and you start telling friends and family about moving to Boston shortly. You think that from now on it is going to be a smooth ride towards the beginning of class. Think again! HBS will now introduce you to one of its favorite tools: the HBS online checklist. It's the tool that ensures HBS that you will be ready with everything by the time the school wants it to be done.

---

27 HBS claims to provide some kind of financial assistance to 65% of its students. Find out more about the financial aid options at HBS at **http://goo.gl/FO8HwR**

28 This is rare – most companies that do this seem to be Japanese?!?

29 I will not dive into the details of this, as it is very dependent on your personal situation, background and nationality. There are a lot of online resources though that can help you with this. And don't forget to try and speak to HBS alums from your country who will know some of the financing channels available to you.

This first checklist is part of the prematriculation[30] website of HBS – one that is fully dedicated to preparing the future MBA students for their two year program. The prematriculation website provides information on the items around a central checklist. This first checklist has no less than 34 items to be completed before arriving on the HBS campus in the fall. It contains items such as 'Send official transcripts', 'Complete HBS Classcards', 'Watch diversity video' and 'Configure HBS wireless network'. Each item on the checklist features detailed deadlines and instructions.

Some items on the list can be very time-consuming; some even include exams. There are tutorials in accounting, finance and quantitative analysis that take about 10 to 15 hours each to complete – according to an estimate provided by HBS. Like most students, I initially skimmed the hours-long tutorials and dramatically failed my first attempts at the online exams[31] which followed. So here you are, having a full-time job and a couple of tutorials taking somewhere between 10 to 15 hours each on some of the 'most exciting topics ever' like accounting and finance. You just failed your first attempt at the exam (out of a max of two attempts, as stipulated) for two of the e-learnings. You are not sure about what will happen if you fail at both attempts, but you sure as hell don't want to be the one to find out.

So what do you do? You sweat, study, and go over the materials again and again. In the end, just one hour before the deadline at 2AM in the timezone I was at that time, I successfully completed all of my e-learnings. But it was a close one! I later chatted with some of my fellow students on how hard some of the tutorials were – most of them agreed, but no one said (or admitted for that matter) they failed both exams.

---

30 If you are confused by the word 'prematriculation', so was I. According to dictionary. com, this word nor its variant 'pre-matriculation' actually exists! It seems that graduate schools have invented it by combining the words 'pre' and 'matriculation', with the latter meaning something like 'being admitted to a group'. As such, prematriculation here means as much as 'before being admitted to a group', or to use the HBS terminology of it, something like 'complete all of these checklist items or you are out!' I invite you to look up 'what does prematriculation mean' on Google and see for yourself!

31 The tutorial exams typically consist of multiple choice questions that have little or nothing to do with the case-based type of education HBS likes to brag about. A typical question would ask you about the book value of a certain transaction you just did as a business owner. A typical transaction would be buying a company car, with additional charges linked to sales tax, registration fees and the cost of a full tank of gas. How many of these transactions would be reflected on your financial books?

Checklists remain a HBS darling in the two years to come. They would appear for other programs such as FIELD2, recruiting activities, EC class selection[32] and finally graduation. But I might as well have forgotten about some other ones. The checklists were also a clear indicator of how HBS has everything tightly under control. Big brother is tracking you... one item at a time...!!!

---

32 EC stands for Elective Curriculum – EC year refers to the second school year at HBS during which courses can be freely elected by students. This in contrast to the RC year – Required Curriculum – which refers to the one-size-fits-all first school year at HBS.

PART

II

GETTING AROUND:
THE FIRST COUPLE OF
WEEKS AT HARVARD

9

Made it to Cambridge?... On your marks, get set,...

HOLD ON! Before the real start of classes at HBS, there are tons of activities arranged to get to know your fellow classmates. The earliest of these opportunities are HBS's pre-MBA programs, which are offered to students in the weeks prior to the start of the MBA program. There are two of these programs. The first is targeted at international students, as most of them come from different educational systems and lack exposure to the academic experience in the U.S. As part of this program, which is available at an additional cost, students get first-hand exposure to life as a student at HBS and what to expect from a learning experience predominantly based on class discussions. The second pre-MBA program focuses on helping students without a business background to get up to speed in preparation for their business training on themes such as finance.

While I did not attend the pre-MBA courses, most students who attended those programs were very positive about them. More than advertising the content of the course itself, they were positive about the early networking opportunities. Upon arrival in a new country, city and environment, the pre-MBA provided a good kick start to meet new people. Most of the pre-MBA friendships last throughout the MBA program, and maybe even well after that.[33]

In addition to the pre-MBA, there are a wide variety of social events scheduled as part of the regular beginning of the program. The Student Association at HBS organizes drinks and brunches students can sign up for. Students are split into random groups, then given a time and a location to meet. You would walk into a restaurant or pub in search of the HBS group you would network with that day. I admit I felt skeptical about these blind date meetings with random people at first as it felt somewhat outside of my comfort zone. However, these meetups ended up being fun and a great

---

33 HBS has made changes to the pre-MBA programs recently, shifting part of the class experience of those programs to online courses. This might undermine the social aspects of the program.

way to get to know fellow students. And for those who wonder – no, HBS did not pick up the bill for these…

The most memorable pre-HBS activity for me was the White Party on the HBS campus, just a couple of days before the start of school. The deal with the White Party is that everyone comes dressed in white, which is harder than one might think. I had never heard of a White Party prior to going to HBS, so I did some research online on what to expect. Unfortunately, I could not find many resources on the topic. So I figured I would just go all white. Going through my limited wardrobe in the U.S. (all the stuff that fit into the two suitcases that I had brought with me from Europe), I quickly realized that I didn't have what it took to make that work. Together with my girlfriend we headed for the nearest mall to shop for a pair of white pants and a shirt[34]. It was my first investment in clothing for HBS parties, with much more to come in the next two years.

Upon arriving at Spangler lawn, a huge stretch of grassland in the middle of the campus, I remember noticing the size of the crowd, the stage with the big screen behind it, and some people that were not dressed all that white (or else they were totally colorblind). It was my first HBS mass event, and one that was open to partners as well, so I also had my girlfriend with me. Most of the evening was spent eating snacks, hopping from one small group of people to another, getting to know some of them a bit better and trying to remember as many names as possible (something that I am in general not good at to begin with). It was also the evening I was introduced for the very first time to the HBS alcohol bracelet.

Indeed, the waiters at the white party did not give me a beer without having a bracelet. Drinking for those below 21 is illegal in the U.S. – and all measures are put in place to ensure that no one below that age has access to alcohol. I had to go to a stand where my ID was checked before I received my bracelet. I could then finally have my beer for the night. The bracelet turned out to be common practice on all HBS mass events serving alcohol.

---

34 I also had to invest in white underwear – colored underwear under white pants is a no no.

After a couple of beers, it was time to head home. I enjoyed my first evening amongst the entire student body, but also felt a bit nervous about what was to come. Would I be able to fit in with this bunch of people? How many of these people would I frequently hang out with? And most of all, would I be able to wear or use my newly acquired fully white outfit ever again? Then came Monday August 27th 2012 – the real start of the HBS MBA program. 900 newly admitted students gathered in Burden Auditorium for the very first time. I took a random empty seat and made some small talk with the people around me before Dean Nohria took the stage and welcomed us at HBS. The screen behind him projected a short and simple message: "Welcome class of 2014." Here I was at the start of an exciting new adventure. Game on HBS!

10

Welcome aboard your MBA program
– meeting your section

An MBA class at HBS is huge – every year, 900 newly admitted students start their life-changing experience in Boston. And while every single one of the 899 other students can be considered your peers, 89 of them will become a much bigger part of your HBS experience. First year students are grouped into sections of 90, ranging from section A to J. Some say there's also a section X – more on that later.

Students will share most of their experiences with this group of 90. The assignment to sections is done by the HBS administration, and rumors say that a lot of time and effort is put into cutting the student body across sections to ensure gender/race/professional/age diversity in all sections. However, most of it seemed rather random to me.

Sections have been around for decades. And while there is no link between the students that are assigned to a certain section today and the students that have graduated from that section in the past, the school goes a long way to instill what I would call section pride. Students have to be proud of their section – and the school encourages this section camaraderie through creating a mild sense of competition between sections[35].

It was not until the first day of school that I would find out who my section mates would be. We all gathered in what would be our home for the next year, Aldrich 109. Upon entering this room, I quickly looked for what would be my seat for the next couple of months. Row 4, two seats in, there was a name tag with my name on it! As I sat down and looked over the HBS classroom, I fell in love with my spot straightaway. I always love to have a view. And things got even better when two lovely ladies sat down on either side of me. What were the chances in a class with only 40% women!

After some small talk with the people around me, class started. Our section coordinator, part of the HBS professor staff, gave a short introduction, and then we were to introduce ourselves one by one. People described their families, their backgrounds, what they did before school and what they would like to do after school. Some were calm, others super nervous. Some were funny, others dead serious. It was such a stream of information that I could barely remember any of it. But I knew it didn't really matter, as I would spend a lot of time with these people in the coming months so I'd get to know them all.

Only later did I come to realize how intense the section experience really was. As a section, you develop a certain habit of working together. Unspoken and unwritten rules develop. You also start knowing what to expect when someone is about to speak during class. As a section, you will also start building a reputation. Section A is the section with all the fun people. Section B gradually evolved toward being the party section. And my section, section C? Well, I think most students saw our section as one with a lot of interesting and nice people. And after spending two years with them, I fully concur with that statement!

---

35 They create competition by showing statistics of the performance of each section. These could range from grade statistics to the outcome of inter-section simulation exercises. Later on, the school would leverage on this competition to drive donations to the school – which section donates the highest amount of money?

11

Finding your home in the HBS classroom

Most of the HBS classrooms in the Aldrich building look exactly the same. They consist of five rows of seats spread in three sections separated by aisles leading to the exit doors. Students have a nickname for each of these rows – the lowest level is called the wormdeck and the upper level is called skydeck. Skydeck offers the best view and the best opportunity to see what is going on in class, which is an advantage that is helpful for pranks and jokes – more on this later!

Seating in the first year at HBS is assigned by the administration and is fixed for a full semester. A new seat will be assigned for students at the start of the second semester. I was very happy with my first seat at HBS. I was relatively high up in the room and could therefore get away with being distracted or doing other things in class (one can't be fully focused all of the time, right?)[36]. I also had good visibility of the class and the boards.

My second semester started off trickier – I was assigned to the worm-deck, the lowest row of the class. This meant I had the professor walking right in front of me all of the time, on top of having to look up to the board and not having any visibility on what was going on behind me. I hated wormdeck – and I got lucky one month into the second semester, when one of my classmates with a skydeck seat asked if I was willing to swap seats for the remainder of the year. He was about to undergo eye surgery which would affect his eyesight for a couple of weeks. I was delighted, and returned to a seat with a view… and some privacy!

HBS class seating is about more than just having a place with a view or having a certain amount of privacy. It can also be a strong enabler to your ability to participate in class. Some seats are more conveniently located in the professor's line of sight and can increase your chances of getting called on. Read more about this later.

---

36 Most of the time, this involved preparing cases for the next day. At one point in time, I even devoted some of my time in class to studying Japanese.

Seating in the second year at HBS is a very different ballgame. Students do not attend all classes with the same group of students anymore. Instead they shop for the classes they have an interest in. As such, students now move from one room to another in between classes, having different students around them every class. Seats are not assigned by HBS at this point – rather, one week into the semester, students get to keep the seat they have at that moment. It is not surprising that 'seat day' often starts pretty early for a lot of people who are trying to secure some of the best seats in the house. I came one hour early for class on seat day just to make sure I could have a seat with a view and privacy – up high in class, preferably in the middle section. Others, on the other hand, really like the proximity to the professors and the board, so taste does matter.

But once you have your fixed seat, the process is the same for everyone. Take your name tag, put it in the little slot in front of you and start paying attention in class. And after a while, that spot automatically becomes a new home…

12

HBS Section Retreat – learning the basics of non-academic HBS life

It is an HBS custom to spend a weekend with all of your section mates in a resort in Massachusetts or a neighboring state in the weeks following the start of the MBA program. As with most events at HBS, the date is chosen by the HBS administration. The retreat weekend can best be summarized as a combination of games, parties and a lot of drinking. But most of all, it is a first real opportunity to get to know many of your fellow section mates (and their partners/families) in a totally different setting, far away from the HBS campus and classrooms.

My HBS section spent its retreat in a resort in New Hampshire, on the border of Lake Winnipesaukee. A tent on the beach was the ideal venue for dinner, sportive games such as 'Color wars'[37] and drinking related games such as beer pong[38] and flip cup[39]. Later in the evening, we discovered the singing/musical/dancing talents of some of our section members.

As an international student, I struggled to fully understand all the games. It seemed beer pong was all about throwing ping pong balls into cups filled with beer. Whenever a player managed to throw a ball into one of the cups on the other end of the table, the player of the other team would have to drink that cup of beer. Flip cup was a bit more complicated – with students standing around a table trying to flip their cup around with a finger. If successful at flipping the cup, players stayed in the game. Those failing to flip it, were out of the game and/or had some drinking to do. It was only later that I realized these games are 'big' in the U.S.!

Another popular thing at HBS parties are costumes – the retreat hosted no less than two full-blown dress-up parties. One night was eighties style. The other night was themed 'bright and tight'! I was amazed by the time and energy most people put into finding the perfect outfit for the theme parties, with dozens competing for the 'best costume' prize. To inspire the section, the organizing committee had even sent out links to websites suggesting possibilities for the themes.

While I truly enjoyed the retreat and the time spent with my section mates, I must admit that the most enriching experience for me took place in the weeks prior the retreat. As the retreat is organized before any section officers are in place, this event is typically organized by a 'coalition of the willing'. I was part of this coalition, and found it a very interesting experience. Putting together a weekend for more than 100 people (most section mates with some of their partners and some children), just three weeks out, with a team of ten very competent but very A-type personalities was challenging but also a very good learning experience. We got the location sorted, festivities planned, car-sharing organized and drinks taken care of.

---

37 In color wars, students are split into different teams for games. I was on the
   green team!   39
        38 Find out more here: **http://goo.gl/hsDTn9**
        39 Find out more here: **http://goo.gl/f9GlM2**

On top of that, we had to deal with the HBS administration. They organized some sessions with the retreat organizers of each section to brief them on 'security information' to make sure that nothing 'unfortunate' would happen during the retreat[40].

I guess this is what HBS is all about – experiencing new things with different types of people. This was probably as important as learning 20 business cases in class. And at the same time, we had great fun! I also learned a lot about my leadership style, which clearly is one of inclusion and collaboration.

13

HBS Diversity – or not quite?

HBS likes to market itself as a very diverse school – it wants to go beyond its reputation of being the school of the 3Ms: Mormons[41], Military, and McKinsey[42]. Traditionally, these groups were a very important part of the HBS student body. Today, the focus on diversity is much more important than it was 20-30 years ago. This diversity can be found in a changing composition of students from a race, nationality, gender, socioeconomic, academic, professional and cultural point of view. Even a European like me had to deal with some cultural differences: I didn't even know what beer pong was prior to starting at HBS – how about that for diversity!?!

Over the last couple of decades, the percentage of international students increased vastly at HBS, though it seems to have stabilized at around 33% in recent years. These statistics are published by HBS on their website. However, I would like to question these statistics based on my experiences at HBS. I consider myself a 'fresh-off-the-boat' international student – I

---

40 Being one of the organizers myself, I was rather shocked to hear that I would be held responsible for any wrongdoing even if not directly involved in the wrongdoing myself. Extreme sanctions could include being expelled from school. Bad experiences in previous years had led the HBS administration to be tough about this. These bad experiences include important damages done by students to hotels and some minor accidents to the students themselves.

41 Mormons are a religious group.

42 A consultancy firm that traditionally has had a strong link with HBS.

never lived or studied in the U.S. before starting at HBS. A significant part of the international student body at HBS however already holds undergrad degrees from U.S. schools. Or, for example, they hold a Belarusian passport but have lived in the U.S. since the age of two (!). Others have lived in the U.S. their whole lives but hold a Ghanaian passport. How international are these people really?

I tried to collect some data on the above statement by looking at the students in my section (which I hope to be representative for the HBS student body). I found 49 of them to be American born and raised (or 54%). About 15% would have a strong link to the U.S. (though potentially having an international passport) – 31% would be international students with little or no prior links to the U.S. It seems my section was actually a very international one in the first place, or HBS is really as diverse as it claims to be!

Diversity at HBS is a tough topic. Despite the many different flags hanging at the back of the class, representing the different nationalities present in the classroom, I found my cultural experience at HBS to be mostly an American one, based on the American lifestyle and way of working. This makes sense when looking at HBS's legacy and geographic location. One can tell by looking at the way the curriculum is set up, the way discussions are held in class or the approach of the administration towards ethical issues (where American values tend to be upheld very strongly). It is also visible on a more superficial level, as when Aretha Franklin was about to sing the U.S. national anthem at Harvard graduation. The speaker duly announced her, saying that "Aretha Franklin will be signing YOUR national anthem." Statistically speaking, the YOUR would have only applied to a certain percentage of the crowd in this case…

Another diversity item that has been discussed extensively at HBS is gender equality. This theme was very hot at HBS in 2013, as the school then celebrated W50, or the 50 years that women have been admitted to the school. Over the last 50 years, the pool of women at HBS has grown from a dozen pioneers in 1963 to about 40% of today's class. More on this later.

Finally, there is the socio-economic diversity at the school. An MBA is an expensive undertaking, and there's a valid question to be raised if it is something that is accessible for all. The admissions process at HBS is need-blind, meaning that students are selected based on their merits and not based on their financial means to pay for the schooling. It is only AFTER HBS has admitted someone to its student body that students have to explain their financial status to the school (and that they can apply to HBS scholarships or other means of financial support).

It is hard for me to judge or question the socio-economic diversity of my class. First of all, there is a disproportionate amount of sons and daughters of millionaires (or billionaires for that matter). They are part of a wealthy family, or have parents who have been very successful in their professional lives. On the other hand, there are the children of upper middle class parents, who got the chances they needed in life to excel in their merits – I am part of this crew. And then there are those who came from very humble beginnings. There are those who managed to excel through a career in the military or who stood out through entrepreneurial ventures or strong academic records. I believe though that the majority of people at HBS come from family settings and backgrounds that gave them solid chances in life, though there is a wide gap between those driving a fancy sports car to school every day and those staying in a cheap dorm room. I believe what struck me most was the wide range of social-economic background of the people I met at HBS. This was different from what I experienced in Belgium where I grew up. Disposable income levels there tend to be more similar across the population due to taxation and politics aimed at redistributing part of the wealth. I guess experiencing this wider gap was part of my MBA experience as well.

14

Classroom decorations

The vast majority of the MBA classes are taught in the Aldrich building. This building, right in front of Spangler cafeteria, has about 12 identical classrooms that host each of the sections of the program. As mentioned previously, each section has its own classroom. While all classrooms look exactly alike, one thing that makes them stand out from one another is the classroom decorations.

It has been a tradition for decades for students to 'decorate' their respective rooms. The preferred technique is hanging a flag for every nationality represented in class. The result is a colorful view on some very familiar flags (France, Germany, etc.) and other flags that are less well known (Bhutan, Somalia, etc.).

This tradition has also led to some controversy in recent years – what does one call a country? What should we do if someone wants to put a Taiwanese flag up, knowing that this might upset other (Chinese) students? Or a Basque one (which in turn might upset Spanish students)? HBS has faced issues of this nature in the past, and tried to propose other ways to celebrate the multi-cultural aspect of a classroom, e.g. by having students put up pictures of their hometown instead.

The flags are still omnipresent, however – and I am personally happy about it. I enjoyed having my national flag in the classroom. I also believe the controversy around which flags to display is an interesting one to have. I personally prefer for this discussion to take place rather than just having it all brushed under the carpet. If students at HBS can't have a mature discussion on this topic – who can?

15

Anatomy of a HBS classroom

The typical Aldrich classroom is pretty well equipped. It has a total of three screen projectors and white screens. Professors have nine blackboards that they can move to different positions both manually or automatically. Every professor has a personal TV screen facing him or her on which they can see what is projected on the screen behind them, while facing the students in the room. There is also an overhead projector for professors who like to track comments made by students on the slides as class progresses.

There are about 100 seats in every classroom and each has its own electronic voting pad. The voting system is pretty cool – it allows professors to check the temperature in the room on certain topics. Some professors like to see the action plans chosen by students for a case in the beginning of the class by polling the class. Then they will see how opinions evolve during class by asking the same question again and putting it up for another vote.

Some 'funny guys' use the voting system as a toy. By discretely but repeatedly changing their answer from, say, A to D and back, the bar chart projected on the screen keeps on showing fluctuating results. And I haven't seen a professor who didn't have any trouble decoding the results of 'dancing bar charts'!

With all that technology in the room, all controlled from a central computer (from which other functions such as the lighting can also be controlled), things go wrong from time to time. Luckily, professors can always rely on a tech rep – a student in every section that has been chosen to intervene in case of a technology problem, e.g. a professor struggling to show a video. The tech rep comes in handy for solving problems related to HBS professors with little or no aptitude for technology. And to confirm the typical stereotype – yes, our tech rep was Indian!

It is also important to note what these classrooms don't have windows. Any exposure to the outside world is annihilated. It might be a nice day outside, or there might be a hurricane raging out – it won't make a difference to the students in class. HBS wants the students to channel their focus toward the class discussion.

Finally, there is a high-definition camera built into the back of the room (whether it serves any purpose or is in use is a mystery). It is supposedly used for filming case protagonists when in class – but who can tell!?!

16

Section leadership and section elections

A section in the first year at HBS consists of about 90 students and as with any large group of people, some kind of leadership is required. The section leadership is decided democratically through a system of elections. Hence, in the first couple of weeks of the program, students in every section will engage in a full-blown election campaign for the various leadership roles, with the most glamorous title being the one of section president. A section president represents the section to the HBS administration. He leads the section leadership team, consisting of a variety of roles such as the section treasurer, the alumni rep and the social reps. Other more exotic roles include the orientation rep (help out with applicants or prospective students who come to campus to sit in on a class), the historian (take and share as many pictures as possible of the section) and the Senator (representing the section in the HBS Student Association). There are a total of 20 leadership roles[43] per section of 90 students – hence 22% or almost a quarter of students in the section have some kind of leadership role.

I applied for the role of section president myself, and have to acknowledge that I failed dramatically. I learned a lot from the experience. One doesn't simply win elections by doing the right thing or being a nice guy (how naïve could I be...). One has to think about clever campaigning, getting people on your side, and most importantly convincing those who really don't care about the outcome of the election to put in the smart vote.

I remember that a couple of days before the election, our future president approached me. He offered to form an alliance with me. Being one of the top three contenders for the section presidency, he wanted to make

---

43 The list of all 20 section leadership positions: Section President / Senator / Education Rep / Leadership and Value Rep / Section Social Chair (2) / Treasurer / Admissions Rep (2) / Alumni Rep / Athletic Rep / Career Rep / Harbus Rep / Historian / International Rep / Orientation Rep / Student Association (SA) Social Rep / Service Rep / Technology Rep / Women's Student Association (WSA) Rep.

sure that the 'loser' could still have a spot in the section leadership later on. A very clever move from him – one that should have warned me about how serious he was about the presidency. While I focused on preparing a strong position paper and a convincing speech to the section, he played the political game to gather the most votes. The experience was very valuable – and looking back at it now, I am very happy that the other guy won. He was an amazing president. He was much more the leader the section needed, than I would have been.

After the election, he kept his promise and offered me a position in the section leadership. I gratefully thanked him for it, but I wanted to respect the outcome of democracy and declined the offer. The tricky thing with section elections is that you can only run for one role. If you lose the election for that role, you can't take up any other leadership role. It adds to the complexity of deciding which roles to apply for.

I hereby want to thank my section leadership. They all did an amazing job in making the section an unforgettable experience! Thanks!

17

Living in the USA

My time at HBS was not only about pursuing an MBA – it was also about experiencing life in the U.S. for two years. One might think that the U.S. and (continental) Europe are very similar, yet I was struck by the differences between the two continents.

First there were the obvious differences. I was surprised by the poor state of most of the infrastructure, with roads and airports in need of urgent upgrades and solid rail connections almost inexistent. I found the hundreds of intertwined electricity cables hanging above my head in most streets in Cambridge resembling the electricity network of a developing country. I was shocked by the poor insulation in most of buildings and the lack of progress fixing this despite the hot and humid summers and the horribly cold winters in Boston.

On the positive side, I was often impressed by the can-do attitude of most Americans. I felt there is a much stronger sense of meritocracy compared to Europe – work hard and you will succeed! People are more open to taking risks and think big. Being wealthy is an aspiration and is viewed with admiration.

And then there were the small differences. As much as I tried, I just couldn't make sense of measurements such as feet and inches and relied on the good old metric system. I was condemned with rather confusing recipes asking for things like a tablespoon of sugar and a cup of milk (which are both official measures). And I had a hard time printing older documents drafted in A4 standard size on a smaller letter size used in the U.S. And what does 90 degrees Fahrenheit feel like?

Finally, I struggled when ordering something in a bar or a restaurant. When asking for a beer, I had to choose a specific type (draft or bottle? Budweiser, Miller, Heineken, Corona, Hoegaarden...?). The same issues arose when ordering pasta (what kind of cheese would you want with that?) and the accompanying salad to it (normal, special, caesers...?) each with their own options of dressing (oil and vinegar, mustard... you name it!) before finally having to decide on the tip you will leave behind for service. Once decided on leaving a 15% tip, you're just left with calculating 15% out of $63.48 and you're all set! I feel that in Europe, choices are much more limited and left to the chef's palette...

At the end of the day, both the U.S. and Europe have pros and cons – and I am very happy that I got to experience the best of both worlds. Now I just need to remember that an inch is about 2.5 cm and that I can wear a shorts and flip flops when it's 90 degrees outside...

PART
III

HBS 'ROUTINE'

18

HBS timing... When? Where? What?...

The first couple of weeks at HBS feel like starting a new job at a new company. You barely know what's going on. You are not sure about when to show up where. And you are struggling with all kinds of acronyms. It's at that point that you start looking for some helpful tools to navigate you through this new maze. What saved me during my first couple of weeks at HBS was the HBS calendar – an online calendar uploaded by the HBS administration. This calendar contained all of my mandatory classes and events. In each of the calendar invites, there was a link to an online repository system with a digital copy of the case for that class and a standard set of questions. Conveniently, this calendar could be synched to your phone and/or PC.

On top of the mandatory events, there are (literally) hundreds of other events going on at the HBS campus or at surrounding schools. These events range from afternoon talks and HBS club events to section sports activities. While it seems almost impossible to describe all the ins and outs of what a typical HBS week looks like (and no two weeks are the same) I thought of sharing a screenshot of my HBS calendar to give you an idea[44]. All the orange calendar entries are events organized by the HBS administration and are mandatory to attend (mostly classes). The other ones are optional events I signed up for[45].

Note that the typical day at HBS in the first year starts at 8AM with a 'discussion group' (more on that in the next chapter). Also note that my agenda is packed with light blue events – or non-mandatory events that I signed up for and/or downloaded to my calendar. Students receive daily emails summarizing events on or around campus. Students can have a

---

44   Find calendar screenshot here: **http://goo.gl/mmDjEJ**
45   You might notice that there are A LOT of events in the calendar – with quite a lot of them overlapping. This is because of the typical HBS FOMO (Fear Of Missing Out) – you want to be part of as much of the interesting stuff as possible! So you sign up for everything and you'll often decide at the last minute what you end up going to.

look at the events and download invites to their calendar directly from the email. These tools enabled me to properly manage my time, despite the large number of events going on.

I was astonished to hear though that the HBS calendar (and the ability to sync it to your phone) had only been around for a year prior to my arrival at school. I don't know how I would have gotten around in my first weeks at HBS without it. And even after that initial period, these IT tools would remain crucial. Thank you HBS for making my life easier. And respect to those in prior generations who did not have access to these tools. But then again, there was a time when even I managed to survive without a smartphone, right?

19

The 8AM test-run – the HBS discussion groups

The HBS educational model is fully based on the case method. This method can be a bit overwhelming for some, as it is very different from the textbook lecture models used elsewhere[46]. On top of that, classes at HBS cover a wide range of topics and industries, exposing students to problem sets they might not be familiar with. A day at HBS could start with a class on a company facing a supply chain issue, followed by dealing with ethical questions in the pharmaceuticals industry, and ending with an in-depth financial problem-set.

With students at HBS coming from all kinds of backgrounds, some will struggle with the hard finance cases (I did!), while others will struggle with topics related to supply chain. To help students out, HBS introduced the discussion groups, in which students can share experiences and knowledge on the cases, so students are well-prepared for the topics of the day. Students are assigned to a group of six across sections, who have to meet

---

46 The typical academic model is different. It normally involves a professor lecturing a classroom filled with hundreds of students. The professor does all the talking – the students listen and take notes. This model is very different compared to the one used at HBS, where students do most of the talking.

every morning at 8AM. During these discussion groups, students prepare for the class discussion later that day.

I had very different experiences with my discussion groups. My first one (assigned by HBS) was great. We were all different but very complimentary. The wake-up often felt too early, but our discussions enriching and our time spent together even more so. I learned about the cases, but I mostly learned about entrepreneurship in the developing world (Elisa), what it meant to grow up as a gay person in a conservative part of the U.S. (John) and the challenges linked to working for the Democratic Party in the run-up to presidential elections (Liz)[47].

After the first couple of months, HBS mixed up the discussion groups. And all of a sudden, my 8AM meetings became a torture. There was no magic between my new discussion group and I. Many of them often turned up late or not at all. There was little or no real collaboration. Our morning discussions were just about comparing our financial models to check if our answers were aligned. Cases that didn't require any modeling or hard numbers (which is a big part of the cases) were not even discussed – most of my new discussion group members considered that pointless. It was a very different experience from before, and I missed the intense discussions of my first discussion group more than ever.

Discussion groups are not mandatory after the first semester. HBS encourages students to create their own, but the school doesn't allocate any longer[48]. After the bad experience with my last group, I was doubtful about joining a new one. Luckily, I was contacted by some people that were in my first discussion group, combined with some like-minded souls. It was a great experience all over again! I learned about the challenges of improving the educational system in the U.S. (Katherine), the amazing road to getting a top consultancy job (Karen) and the complications involved with resigning from a Korean company (Ying). I loved every bit of it – and every single one of them.

The reality is that my experience might have been very different from most. A lot of people give up on their discussion groups quickly – how do

---

47 Names have been changed for privacy reasons.
48 You can request that the HBS administration assign you to one, however.

you motivate a group of six young HBS students to meet at 8AM in the morning every day with classes only starting at 9.10[49]? But I kept snoozing to a minimum and took as much from this 'sharing to grow' principle as I could… and I loved it! The discussion groups became almost as important to me as the classes themselves. While classes are based on a discussion model between students, not all student gets to speak in every class[50]. With limited opportunities to actually speak in class, the discussion groups provided the ideal platform to practice putting a point across! And of course, I very much so enjoyed the occasional croissant breakfast with my group!

20

Cold feet for the HBS cold call

The MBA program at HBS is fully case-based. Students prepare a case before class and discuss all aspects of the case in class. The professor has the role of facilitator and specialist. As these discussions are such an important part of the teaching method at HBS, students' grades depend heavily on class participation. Most of this class participation is voluntary, as students get called on by the professor after raising their hand. There is however one exception to this rule – the HBS cold call.

The anatomy of a cold call goes something like this: the professor walks into class and says, "Johnny, can you tell me what the case is about today?" Then the professor and the chosen student will spend the first 5 to 10 minutes of class discussing the case, the protagonist and the actions that he/she should take. To some students, cold calls are a big source of stress. To others, they are a much needed motivator to prepare each and every case. And then there are those who just seem to master the art of "talking their way out" of any difficult situation and don't consider the cold calls as a threat.

---

49 Further complicated by the fact that students are often up late studying or partying or both…

50 A typical class lasts for 80 minutes. With 90 students in class, it is likely to only have 20 to 25 different students actually speak in class.

Not all cold calls are the same… they can differ massively between professors. Find my "HBS cold call survival guide" below.

1. The very very very random cold call

They do exist – the professors that make their cold calls totally random. One professor guarantees total randomness for the cold call by throwing a dart at the class seating chart. Anyone is welcome to witness his dart skills the day before class at 10AM in his office. At the start of class, he will go up to the student who ended up being the "bull's eye", show him the hole in the seating chart paper and start questioning him as part of the cold call. One downside of randomness – the same student can be cold called multiple times… or even twice in a row! There just doesn't seem to be a way to avoid a potential call. My advice: make sure you have a seat on the outer limits of the classroom – his darts don't seem to make it to that area very often. Or head over at 10 AM every day to the professor's office to see if you got 'darted'.

2. The supposedly random cold call

While most cold calls seem random, many of them actually have some level of predictability. Not all professors perform the darts procedure or pick a random student in class. Be aware that it's often students who don't speak a lot in class who get targeted by professors. Bad news for the silent ones, good news for the active ones. Avoid these cold calls by making the occasional voluntary comment in class… and as such avoid a potential cold call on a tough day.

3. The supposedly predictable cold call

Other professors put a lot of effort into picking their cold calls. At HBS, professors need to know their students' names, backgrounds, and specifics. They gather this information from the HBS classcards, an online tool updated by HBS students with their general information, professional background and a set of additional random facts. This information is supposed to help professors steer discussions in class based on people's expertise. One professor took this part of his job very seriously. At the beginning of every class, he would walk through his reasoning of how exactly he chose today's cold call victim. He would begin with stating some obvious relationship between a student and the case of the day. He would then reason through a sequence of links based on students' classcards to finally arrive at a student that would seemingly otherwise be unrelated to the case, nearly giving several students a 'heart attack' in the process. As an example, he would call on a person who likes to travel to comment on a case on Airbus. However, stating that this link was too obvious, he would go for the student that has all of the letters of Airbus in their name… or to the French student in class since Airbus is mainly French. My assessment – keep the "additional information" field in the classcard as empty as possible to avoid links to cases.

4. The "I-thought-I-was-safe" in-class cold call
While most cold calls happen at the start of class, some professors like to keep attention levels high by calling on random people during class. I have seen this happen most of the time in finance classes… as a lot of people happily let go of the discussion once the cold call has passed. I only have one piece of advice in this case: prepare your (finance) cases!

5. The "Oh crap!" cold call
So you are sitting in class and start shaking your head. You do this because a) you were thinking about that great song you heard on the radio earlier OR b) you totally disagreed with a statement of a fellow classmate. Whatever the reason, this kind of reaction can get you a call by the professor even without you raising your hand (as the professor would think you have an opinion you want to share). In this same category, we find the "stretching-in-class-and-the-professor-thinks-you-were-raising-your-hand" call. My advice – always keep a low profile.

6. The non-existent cold call
Only seen in the second year at HBS… where some professors indeed never cold call. However, this is an exception to the rule.

Summary
I would like to emphasize the value of the above advice and I have data to prove it. When making some 'back-of-the-envelope' calculations, a student

at HBS has a chance of being cold called seven times over the 2 years of the MBA program[51]. I was cold called five times at HBS – well below average! I totally failed one of them, did poor on another one and nailed the other three. However, this still remains a pretty low success rate (knowing that I did a good job in preparing my cases 85-90% of the time), which leaves me wondering if the cold calls are maybe not all that random – can the professors smell a lack of preparation?!?!

21

HBS cases – don't miss your intro! And don't forget to prepare your case!

HBS is not only a business school; it is also an important publisher with many business books authored and published by HBS folks. And who hasn't heard of Harvard Business Review? Among students and professionals however, HBS is mostly known for their business cases. Worldwide, they are commonly used as the backbone of trainings given in both academic and business environments. It's no wonder that, although other institutions and business schools are also in the case-creation business, the vast majority of business cases used at the HBS MBA program are from HBS.[52]

HBS cases are accessible to all – in fact, they can be purchased online[53]. Students at HBS have easy access to all HBS cases (even the huge amount of cases not used in class) – they can be requested free of charge in Baker library.

HBS cases tend to follow a typical structure, starting off with a general introduction followed by an overview of historical facts and events. The next section will dive into the actual business problem on hand. The case

51 Two academic years at HBS, each with 30 class-weeks and on average 10 classes a week – 2*30*10=600 potential cold calls. Divide this by the number of students per class = 90, and you have an average chance of being cold called seven times throughout your time at HBS.
52 There are the occasional Stanford or INSEAD cases that come up along the way.
53 Find out more at: **http://goo.gl/XUmkqJ**

will often end on an open note (what does the CEO have to do?) followed by some exhibits that contain detailed data and other relevant information. The average HBS case has about 10 pages of text and 5 pages of exhibits.

It is a running joke that the opening sentence of each and every HBS case is the same – reading something like: "The CEO of company X was looking out of the window of his Manhattan office, reflecting on his next steps to tackle the problem his company had been facing." In more recent cases however, case writers seem to have used their writing skills in the case openings, and a wave of creativity has hit the opening paragraph of cases like never before. There's also a new trend of starting the cases with a strong quote. Finally, I always wondered how much guidance is given to case-writers on writing cases. Do they have to take into account the fact that a vast majority of readers are non-native English speakers? Are they trained in using writing techniques that focus on readability of the content? Do they have guidelines as to how much they can or are allowed to deviate from what really happened to turn the case into solid learning material?[54]

Reading cases is an important part of the HBS experience – hence it is refreshing to have a variety of case writing styles. On average, students have to prepare three cases per day. This adds up to 30 pages of text to read and another 15 pages of exhibits. Extrapolate that to a full week, and students will read the equivalent of a solid book every five days. The intensity of this cannot be underestimated. Moreover, reading is not enough – students need to make sure that they absorb the content, or that they can at least reproduce part of it in class. Here's where students use different techniques. Note that HBS does not allow technology in class (such as laptops or iPads), so the only reference students have is a printed copy of the case.

First, there are those who turn their cases into coloring books. They highlight case facts in yellow, data in pink, and interesting quotes (to be repeated in class) in blue. In the end their cases look Picasso-esque. For them

---

54 I got the chance to ask a case writer some of these questions. First, they are indeed trained in a specific case writing technique. This includes acknowledging that many of their readers are non-native English speakers; therefore it is necessary to use simple vocabulary. Second, they are taught to make the case as engaging as possible, not a dry academic text. Finally, case writers do try to stick to the facts as much as possible. The only time they divert from reality is when the featured company does not want to disclose certain facts.

however, they are a structured source of reference. Personally, I can only imagine how much time and energy the whole coloring thing must take. And what happens when you run out of pink highlighter ink?

Second, there are the virgin cases. These seem untouched – no notes, no tags, no underlined paragraphs. Nothing. These students either don't read cases, make notes on separate pages or have the ability to memorize everything. I am not a virgin.

Third, there are the cases with underlined pieces of text. This was the strategy I developed. I underlined parts that I deemed important. If I thought I would have to reference them in class, I would also put a line in front of the paragraph – this would allow me to quickly find important pieces of information. Finally, I made sure to have two or three bullet points written on the first page of my case. These would summarize my key thoughts and came in handy in case I was cold called.

The amount of reading was overwhelming at times. Moreover, for international students, having to read in your non-native language makes it even more intense. Despite this, and despite the fact that not all cases were written in the most exciting of ways, I did enjoy spending evenings and nights going through dozens of pages of business problems. Every case was a story taken out of real life with real problems of real people. For some, I had strong opinions. For others I did not have a preferred outcome. But every single case was informative in one way or another, and reading all those stories in the cases made me dream of becoming the protagonist of an HBS case myself. Maybe one day somebody will write a case about this guy who wrote a book on HBS? Who knows… I might become the 'informative required reading' for hundreds of HBS students one day…

22

HBS punctuality – "Better three hours too soon than a minute too late" (Shakespeare)

Rumor goes that Dean Nohria, when still part of the teaching staff at HBS, had his own techniques to ensure all students arrive on time for his classes. He would start his class as most professors do with a cold call, then move on to open the debate in class.

However, where most professors ignored students coming late to class (and sneaking to their seat), Professor Nohria was said to explicitly welcome that person into class. He would then start class all over again for the latecomer (even as far as starting with a new cold call!)[55]. Needless to say that it only took a couple of classes for all students to arrive on time.[56]

Punctuality is key at HBS. Classes start on time.[57] (I never had a professor come late for class – ever!). Other HBS events are equally punctual. Anything driven by the HBS administration will start and end on time. The discipline demonstrated by HBS is impressive – and I believe it is a good habit to have. Interestingly so, this seems a very Harvard/HBS point of focus, as I have often heard about classes at other schools or other programs starting late.

However, informal meetups amongst students (whether it being for social reasons or to work on common projects) are often much less punctual. As I grew up in a family where punctuality matters, I did like how HBS focused on having classes start on time. I do believe punctuality matters and loved how HBS enforced it. As to my personal contribution toward HBS timeliness, I admit I was late once (by four minutes – I overslept…) for one class over my two year MBA program. I am sure even William Shakespeare would forgive me for that one.

---

55 This was way before my time at HBS. I only have this from hearsay.
56 I've heard from students at INSEAD that late-comers have to pay a fine – the funds collected go straight into the 'Champagne Fund'!
57 Students automatically stop talking to each other seconds before class starts.

23

Is it really only cases?

A couple of months into school, I started to wonder if HBS was keeping to its promise with regard to the value of its MBA program. However, it was difficult to quantify 'future career prospects' or the 'dynamism of the student life' and the 'valuable networks' that it forms[58]. I did find a way to verify another HBS MBA promise: the HBS academic experience. On their website, HBS describes the value of the academic part of the HBS MBA experience as follows: "Through case method courses, FIELD projects, multimedia simulations, and more, you'll exercise the leadership skills you will practice in business and beyond." Here's how I tried to validate this by analyzing the events in my calendar from my first semester at HBS.

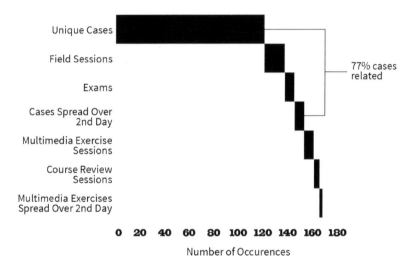

HBS academic planned workload – by occurrence

---

58 These are all claims from HBS as stipulated on their website.

Over the course of the semester, I had 168 mandatory academic HBS events in my calendar. More than 3/4 of them were related to business cases discussed in class, as one would expect from an HBS MBA program. I was exposed to a total of 120 unique business cases taught over 129 sessions in just 16 weeks. Apart from the cases, 18 sessions were dedicated to FIELD and/or section norm reviews. The FIELD program at HBS aims to help students to become more collaborative, more global and more 'hands-on'. In short, FIELD1 is about improving teamwork, FIELD2 aims at a business experience in an international setting, while FIELD3 pushes students toward addressing the entrepreneurial aspects of business by having them launch a start-up from scratch. Finally, a total of 8 sessions were dedicated to that third HBS promise: multimedia course exercises.

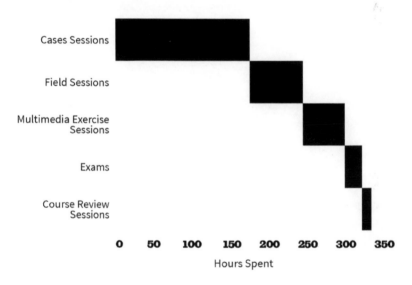

HBS academic planned workload – by time spent

When evaluating the time dedicated to each of these sessions, the balance starts to shift. While cases dominate the number of events, only 50% of the time spent in a classroom environment is dedicated to them. While lower in number, the FIELD sessions are often planned over a whole day and as such represent almost a quarter of HBS academic time. As a comparison, a typical business case class at HBS is 80 minutes long. Finally, we spent a total of 48 hours on the course multimedia exercise sessions.

In summary, I spent 330 hours on the HBS academic experience over the first 16 weeks, the equivalent of 70 days (if you take out days planned for recruiting events and for holidays etc.). A quick calculation brings that to a little less than five hours a day. Add that to a couple of hours a day preparing for class, HBS club meetings and the social events, and the whole HBS experience gets pretty busy! Finally, the exams add to the workload. For the record, my first semester exams at HBS were spread over 9 sessions, totaling about 32 hours (or almost 10%), a surprisingly big chunk of the overall time spent at HBS! In summary, the HBS MBA is more than just about cases. The academic promise of HBS seems to hold up to my research!

24

The HBS class scribes – terror or blessing in disguise?

The HBS class scribes were introduced to support professors in improving their efficiency when calling on people in class. Their initial role was to ensure that professors would call on students evenly across gender, seating position in class and other factors of diversity. Today however, the role of these scribes seems ever more extensive. The scribes are HBS employees who sit in on every class in the first year at HBS and take note of everything said in class. They record the author of each comment as well as the comment. They then provide the professors with data on who participates a lot in class and who doesn't. It's what they are hired to do, and they are the only ones allowed to have a laptop in class… on which they record all of the above (and which makes them highly recognizable).

A few months into my time at HBS, I got my first bad grade for one of my courses. Only then did I realize the full extent of the work of the scribes. A bad grade at HBS is followed by the professor's detailed analysis of your performance. I was astonished to have him refer to two of my comments from class, ones that he was not pleased with. He quoted them and explained why he was not happy with them. The only possible source to have this kind of information was the scribe. I couldn't believe that the scribes had captured my comments to that level of detail!?!

The scribes not only record most of what is said in class, but also take class attendance and duly take note of latecomers. It is a remarkable investment from HBS to have these people sit in on every class for this purpose. I do see the value of having them record information that enables them to provide feedback to professors, hence ensuring everyone gets the chance to participates in class. I would even go as far as thinking of hiring my own version of a scribe in my future professional environments to see if comments made during meetings come from the same people repeatedly. It would be a value-adding statistic to have. So, shall we settle on calling the scribes a blessing in disguise?

25

Skydeck – putting the "HA!" in "HARVARD!"

No better way to end a hard week of class than with a Skydeck session – a real HBS tradition. Skydeck is the name for the upper row in the Aldrich classroom. Students sitting in that row have the best seats in class to observe everything. They can tell who is not paying attention and who is sleepy after a rough party the night before. Nothing goes unnoticed for those sitting on Skydeck. Hence, every 2 weeks or so, a selection of "skydeckers" come down from their top row seats to the front of the class after the last class on Fridays and take control of the class for the next 30 minutes to summarize their observations.

The bi-weekly Skydeck session can best be described as a comedy show about life at HBS. Fellow students, professors and even other sections: everyone is part of the satire of Skydeck. I will not share any detailed content here, as most of it is very situation-specific, but I can assure you that the content of Skydeck was often brilliant. The sketches performed by our fellow students were hilarious and very recognizable for the everyday student at HBS.

I loved the Skydeck sessions – it was our 30 minutes of fun at the end of a week packed with classes and cases. It was the best summary ever of what had been going on for the last two weeks in class. And from time to time, the "skydeckers" would go the extra mile. In some of their presentations, they included videos with professors joining in the fun. For others, they brought music/dancing/party into the classroom. And some Skydeck sessions even went fully digital[59]!

26

HBS clothing – dress to impress

On my first day at HBS, our section coordinator gave a typical start-of-the-year speech. His introductory talk to our HBS experience was followed by a Q&A session, during which one of my brave section mates asked if there was a dress code for students in HBS classes. The coordinator, a tenured professor at HBS dressed in an impeccable tailor-made suit, replied that while he was very much so in favor of a dress code for students (preferably enforcing suits and ties in the process), unfortunately most of the faculty did not share his point of view. There was no formal dress code at HBS, though he politely asked us to show up for class decently dressed.

It was no surprise that many of the shirts and fancy shoes that most students wore to their first day of class were replaced by T-shirts and flip flops the following day. This made the day-to-day dress code at HBS not that different from what people wore outside of class. Nevertheless, there are a couple of interesting facts about HBS clothing I would like to mention.

First of all, part of the student body enjoys having the school name on their clothing. HBS-branded gear comes in different types, sizes and varieties. Most specialized HBS gear is sold by the HBS Student Association (SA) but can also easily be found in stores around Harvard Square.

---

59 Enjoy a digital version of a Skydeck session here: **http://goo.gl/wwXLL3**

Others enjoy wearing the free branded sweatshirts they got from [PUT CONSULTING FIRM NAME HERE] or the cool T-shirts from [PUT TECH COMPANY NAME HERE].

Second, there is the Section gear – a proud symbol of belonging and an ideal way to show your section colors[60]. It includes fancy items like sunglasses, hats, T-shirts and sport outfits. Section gear tends to be managed through the section leadership and can exclusively be bought by section members and their spouses/children.

And then finally, there are the cultural differences in clothing – here's my chance to dig into stereotypes. Americans tend to wear sneakers to class, Europeans can be trusted to show up in fancy shoes. The Latin-American students get the prize for being most classy. The Asian student body is too diverse to categorize. One thing is for sure, these differences don't go unnoticed.

In summary, MBA students can wear whatever they want to class. But one thing that's definitely true is that we don't see the nice ties and jackets that were common to HBS students back in the seventies. As my first-year section coordinator would say: Those were the days…

27

HBS Class visitors – a long-tail distribution

All first-year students at HBS undertake the same rigorous program, and they do so in their assigned classroom, with their same section-mates. However, the number of class attendees varies from one class to another. This number can decrease because of absentees, but can also increase, thanks to the presence of a special specimen: the HBS classroom guest. As guests are a common part of the HBS class experience, each section tends to have a process to receive them. In my section, guests would typically be introduced by the professor or a fellow section-mate, followed

---

60 My section, section C, was proudly wearing black and yellow – inspired by Wiz Khalifa's famous song.

by a round of applause by all students. Depending on the status of the guest, our section agreed upon different standards – while all guests got a round of applause after being introduced, family members of students would get a standing ovation. This process sometimes led to hilarious situations, as the sum of four family members and three other guests in a class led to a total of 4 standing ovations and 3 rounds of applause, as such delaying the start of class by 5 minutes. On top of that, our section agreed to give a round of applause after a comment of a section-mate whose family sits in on the class. This led to funny situations too, as some professors used this in a clever way. After the applause, they would go up to the family members claiming that "this happens every time he/she speaks." I loved it![61]

HBS guests come from a wide range of backgrounds and nationalities. Their participation levels to class discussions also varies. However, they can be classified in one of four highly recognizable categories. An overview:

Martha – The case protagonist

Martha will pop-up ever so often in class. She is one of the main subjects in a case used in the class and can be a company founder, a CEO, or just someone who was in a specific situation at a point in time which resulted in… a HBS business case. They sit in on class and take the floor in the last 20 minutes to share their perspective on what happened, as well as to take questions from students. As different sections are taught the same class at the same time, Martha might not be physically present in class – but will be broadcasted live in the section room, from a different HBS classroom. I love how unpredictable Marthas can be, as they range from the arrogant company founder to the humble company CEO…or the other way around. Examples of Marthas who were physically present in my section room include Dropbox founder and CEO Drew Houston and Boeing CEO James McNerney. [Clap Clap Clap Clap Clap Clap]

---

61   One Dad was very responsive to a professor doing so. He said: "I know, it sometimes even happens at home at the dinner table!"

James – The prospective student

The James beat the other categories in quantity but tend to be the least memorable of guests. They are interested in an MBA and want to experience a class at HBS. They usually overdress (suit + tie) and only cause excitement in class when he or she has a fellow college alum within the section, leading to a little college-name shouting… [Clap Clap Clap GO BROWN Clap Clap Clap]

Rod & Linda – Family & Friends

Rod & Linda tend to be received with the most welcome. They often resemble one of our section mates and are easily recognizable from their uncomfortable demeanor in class, though some of them clearly enjoy being part of the HBS show! Occasionally, Rod & Linda are family of the professor. [Clap Clap STAND UP Clap Clap Clap Clap SIT DOWN]

John Doe – Mystery guests

Once in a while, a John Doe appears in class. John is not introduced by the professor or a fellow section-mate. They are just a mystery. Not an attendee we get to see much. [Silence]

Guests have the benefit of observing the class. However, with the exception of Marthas, guests are not supposed to speak or to participate in any way during class. After all, they don't pay tuition, right!?!

During my time at HBS, I brought a couple of visitors myself. My parents attended a class (the typical Rod & Linda) and really enjoyed the experience. Later in the year, my brother and his wife visited a class as well. And I once brought a friend from MIT[62] who wanted to see what HBS was all about. Looking at them sitting there reminded me of the time when I was a prospective student being a guest in class. I loved it, and it convinced me to apply to HBS. It was a fun and enriching experience, and one I strongly recommend to anyone wanting to apply to business school. Moreover, getting a round of applause from the business leaders of tomorrow is not something that happens daily, right? Enjoy!

---

62   MIT is short for Massachusetts Institute of Technology – yet another top school in the Boston area.

28

HBS Professors – do they know?

During one of the last classes of my fall semester at HBS, we had a Martha type guest in class (as described in the previous chapter, remember?). She had attentively followed the class discussion, and took the floor for the last 20 minutes of class to share her thoughts and reflections on the case and our comments.

She started by thanking the professor for the opportunity to speak in his class, and then she thanked us, the students, for the interesting class discussion. She added that she was delighted that 'some of us had actually read the case and that others had taken the effort to read it during the class itself.' As I had been ill-prepared that day and read most of the case during class, I felt guilty. But most of all, her comment made me wonder about something bigger: "DO THEY KNOW?" Do HBS professors notice all that's going on among students during a typical 80 minute HBS class? Because in all honesty, it's not all about paying attention…

To ensure the full attention of students, HBS classrooms are designed to minimize distraction. They have no windows. All seats are facing the professor. And HBS professors are coached to be as entertaining as possible. Also, technology is not allowed in class – this means no computers or smartphones. All notes are made using pen and paper – except for the occasional finance class in which students are allowed to use their computers to build Excel models. But despite these efforts, students create their own distractions.

First, there is this thing with smartphones. They are small and can easily be hidden behind the HBS name cards – a great way to check emails from time to time. The more daring students even play the occasional Candy Crush game. Then there are those who just love to play low-tech games, such as the secret word game. Students agree on a secret word prior to class, such as "dinosaur."[63] The first student to use that word twice in a comment in class wins.

---

63 Although my favorite secret word definitely was "Chuck Norris"!

Then there is the 'building on John's comment' game. Students often add to an earlier comment in class, but the goal of this game is to build onto a non-existent comment. In this case, John didn't make any comment in that class, but students refer to a comment of his when addressing the professor. It must be a great source of confusion for professors. Then there are those who fall asleep during class (aka recovering from last night's party) in the most discrete ways[64]. And finally, there is educational distraction, e.g. reading HBS cases in class instead of outside of class.

I am sure I have missed at least a dozen of other types of distraction. The point here is that it is not easy for students to stay fully focused during classes they are not particularly interested in, or led by a professor who is surely brilliant but not all that entertaining. As such, in my opinion, everyone can do as they please, as long as they don't distract others around them. But I can imagine that if professors notice these distracted students, it must further increase the challenge of teaching a HBS class. This in turn might lower the quality of the class and cause other students to lose focus as well. Then again, nobody said being a HBS professor was easy. Dear HBS professors – up to you to entertain us… and teach us valuable lessons while doing so!

On a final note – HBS professors also like to add to the fun – albeit more subtly. There was a finance professor who had his parents in class and, in the middle of the action, suddenly cold called his mom when students got stuck on a problem: "Mom, what do you think?" (the woman nearly had a heart attack). Or there was the Operations Management professor who walked into class during an exam to write the following on the board: "In 1 minute it will be 12:12:12 12/12/12". HBS professor humor I guess…

---

64 Women can cover their face with their long hair for instance. A great way to secretly close their eyes for a while.

29

The HBS paper factory

While all business cases are available online in PDF format, HBS does not allow the use of computers or other forms of technology in class. Many of us read books on our e-readers and magazines on our iPads nowadays, yet students have to carry printed books and case studies. This is a strict HBS policy – and one they do not want to part from. The HBS administration claims that technology might distract students too much from class discussions.

While I am somewhat opposed to the huge amounts of paper/trees that are sacrificed as a result of this, I do understand the HBS rational. As part of my previous employment, I gave a lecture at the University of Lausanne a few months prior to my start at HBS. During my 2-hour lecture, nearly every student had a computer or iPad sitting in front of them. I hated it. I felt like no one paid attention (even though most of them probably took notes on their computer). So as far as the class materials are concerned, piling up print copies might be a necessary evil after all!

30

The rich and famous

HBS does a brilliant job of bringing you closer to the rich and famous. Actually, most of the time it's the other way around. HBS will bring the rich and famous closer to you. Whatever way it is, the rich and famous love to be associated with HBS, and you can take the terminology "rich and famous" quite literally. Whether present on campus as a case protagonist or as a main speaker at a conference, they are loving it! Equally, students love having them around.

Let's start with the rich category. Some made their money by investing money – meet Ray Dalio, one of the world's most prominent investors through his company Bridgewater, an American investment management firm. He gives an afternoon lecture in Burden Hall on how to invest wisely, wearing comfy loose jeans and not a nice suit, as I expected him to. Others made their money online – meet Hiroshi Mikitani, the founder and CEO of Rakuten, one of Amazon's biggest competitors, who will address students during an informal event over dinner.

Then there are the famous ones. Meet Clay Christensen, HBS professor and the guy who gave us the disruption theories[65]. Meet Sir Alex Ferguson, former manager of one of the greatest soccer clubs in history, Manchester United. Or how about having a private demo of magician Jason Randal in class?

And then there are those who are somewhere in between categories, like the CEOs of interesting companies such as Aston Martin and the flamboyant CEO of beer-company Anheuser-Busch Inbev. The founder of Dropbox dropped by, and Jack Welch, former CEO of GE, also popped in. And I am not sure where I would put the politicians from all different parts of the world. But if there's one institute in the world who can bring all of these people together, it must be HBS and Harvard at large!

31

Second year at HBS – last but not least?

I survived both RC (Required Curriculum – the first year at HBS) and EC year (Elective Curriculum – the second year at HBS). As I was about to finish my HBS MBA, I was (choose for yourself) – old / graduated / spoiled for life / happy / super excited to go back to work / broke. But most of all, I was now a real specialist that could shed a light on all aspects of the HBS MBA program, including the comparison between the RC and EC years, and the RC and EC students, typically referred to as RCs and ECs.

Most RCs look at the ECs as the ones with easy lives. HBS seems to be less controlling of their schedules, and they just look so much more (choose for yourself) – cool / relaxed / mature / tanned. As an RC, you just can't wait

---

65 For those interested, find HBS professor Clay Christensen's theories on disruption here: **http://goo.gl/VfvEz1**

to become an EC and enjoy some of the EC perks, which include flexible class schedules and a lower workload. But let's assess things on a deeper level. Find my own personal and subjective comparison of the RC and EC year at HBS below.

Class experience

In the first year at HBS, students are grouped in sections of 90 – all classes are taught within that same group. This also means that students will spend the whole year in the same classroom AND the same seat (seat is changed only once per year). The second year at HBS is very different – students choose their own courses and are thus not attending classes with that same section anymore. They move around from one classroom to another. One tip here: don't forget to take your name-card from one room to another! Overall, the RC section experience is so unique... I have no choice but to give my first point to the RC-year!

Jobs!

RCs look for summer internships; ECs look for full-time jobs! One can quickly understand that this second activity tends to be much more stressful than the first one. Find out more about recruiting at HBS later on. An extra half a point for RC-year!

Grading

With 50% of a course grade based on class participation at HBS, there is still another 50% of the grade dependent on other components. In RC year, this could be an exam at the end of the semester. In EC year, most courses tend to require writing one or more (final) papers. Personally, I prefer exams. A 4-hour exam is just so much less time-consuming than writing a 12-page paper! RC year gets just half a point for this, as I do like the flexibility in time management of writing papers.

Freedom of choice!

As mentioned, the RC year is fixed for everyone – no choice here! In the second year, this changes as students get the opportunity to choose their own courses. And more importantly, every course starts at a different time, so those who tend to be a wreck in the morning can try and avoid these nasty 8.30AM classes! Find more info on EC class selection later! EC year 1 point!!!

Food baby!

So, here's a math question: how long will you have to wait in line for lunch knowing that 900 RC-students all finish their morning program at 12:10 sharp? And how much time can you save in queuing during EC-year when students have more flexible programs with a variety of different class times? Yep, the best thing about being an EC is not having to wait in line for food! EC one point!

With a little help of my friends...

Your first year at HBS can be a confusing and stressful experience. But no worries, HBS makes sure that each section has a leadership team in place to take care of the lost ones. There is a section president, a sports coach, two social chairs, the section CFO (who will eagerly collect the section dues) and much, much more. But most importantly, each section will also have an Educational Rep who sends out reminder mails of important tasks to keep track of. In EC year, you're on your own! Another point for RC!

When the non-HBS crowds roll in...

As everything in RC-year is very much controlled by HBS and the focus is on the section-experience and the section feel, no outsiders are allowed in class, except for the earlier described visitors. In EC-year, HBS allows cross-registrants from different nearby schools, mostly from the Harvard Kennedy School and the Harvard Law School, but also from MIT and other schools in the Boston area. Others are part of leadership programs within Harvard, where people with successful careers come and sit in on certain classes (these people include former Goldman Sachs partners, VC-leaders from Silicon Valley, etc.). As cross-registrants aren't always aware of some of the HBS specificities and rules in the classrooms, they tend to quickly stand out during class[66]. But as far as I am concerned, I love to hear from

66 Find an 'ode' to the HBS cross-registrant here: **http://goo.gl/fz6FRJ**

these people in our classes, as they tend to bring different views and insights. EC-year, one final point!

RC year vs EC year: 3-3

So we got ourselves a 3-3 tie between RC and EC year. Both experiences are impossible to compare – it is the combination of those two very different years that makes the HBS experience what it is! So the real answer here is that both years are great, and if admitted to HBS, you'll get to experience them both anyway! Enjoy!

32

Say Thanks initiative – the new kid on the block!

While HBS orchestrates a lot of initiatives, some come from students themselves. My class of 2014 launched the 'say thanks' campaign. The idea originated when a couple of students realized they knew little or nothing about the women sitting at the cash register in the cafeteria, or the guys wiping the blackboards right after class, or the people providing a lot of support to professors in the background. All those people play an important role contributing to the HBS experience, yet most students barely know of their existence.

A school like HBS couldn't run without all its staff, and some students in my class wanted to do something for those that weren't in the spotlight. They wanted to recognize ALL the staff at HBS, not just the professors. Thus the Say Thanks campaign was born.

I will admit, I was a bit skeptical about this plan at first. My doubts were quickly replaced with respect for the creators of this initiative, as it created a great vibe through the school. Turns out it's great to say thanks to someone. And based on the feedback we gathered from the HBS staff, it is even better to receive thanks. This initiative didn't require big budgets or massive investment. Rather, the Say Thanks initiative was just about making a cute thank you video, or a nicely written thank you card for the HBS staff. The effect was marvelous!

HBS is an institution full of traditions. And ever so often, a new one is created. I believe that the Say Thanks initiative will be embedded in the HBS world. And one day, I will be able to say I saw the birth of what would become an HBS tradition. Find out more on Say Thanks here: **http://goo.gl/GgSep1**

33

Disrupting the routine of the HBS machine – it takes a disaster

Dean Nohria's speech[67] on graduation day of the Class of 2014 summarized it well – my class had faced its share of difficulties during its tenure at HBS. With the students standing in front of him, dressed in their graduation gowns, he called the Class of 2014 a 'disaster resistant' one. And the man had a point. During my 2 years at HBS, I faced several abnormal situations, some of them which would have never occurred in my hometown (I had never experienced a hurricane before for instance). Dean Nohria summarized them as follows:

- Hurricane Sandy severely hit the East Coast of the U.S. (including Boston) in 2012 and was supposedly the second-costliest hurricane in the United States' history. There were some damages to HBS buildings
- There was a campus-wide power outage
- Blizzard Nemo hit Boston in February 2013, leaving about 25 inches / 65 cm of snow behind in just one night
- There was a flood in one of the residence halls
- The month of May 2014 (graduation month) was the coldest month of May ever in Boston. Moreover, flash-floods had been predicted for graduation day
- There was a fire in one of the campus apartments blocks
- There was the Boston marathon bombing and the manhunt that followed the attack

---

67 Find Dean Nohria's speech here: **http://goo.gl/zXNDbv**

Turns out Dean Nohria even left out a couple of other events. In September 2013, the U.S. government went into shutdown mode due to a conflict between the Democrats and the Republicans around Obamacare. All non-essential services provided for by the government were shut down. It was one of the longest government shutdowns in U.S. history[68].

Coming from a region of the world where hurricanes don't occur, the passing of Hurricane Sandy was an intense moment for me. I was surprised by the severity and intensity of the storm. All transportation systems on the East Coast of the U.S. shut down. People were told to stay inside and to stock up with enough food and water in case of power outages. Even Harvard closed down. And where was I? I was out of town that weekend, in a place that happened to be right on the path of the hurricane.

I followed the whole storm on TV and by looking out the window. Once the storm had passed, some parts of the East Coast were licking their wounds, particularly in the New York area. I was fine – I was only impacted by the fact that I couldn't get back to Boston in time for classes. The airlines needed some time to get fully operational after the storm. But the storm had left a deep impression on me. And it was only one of the disasters I had to overcome during my time at HBS…

---

68 For those that want to know how the average American feels about all this, one can always count on Jimmy Kimmel to go out on the street and to ask the right/wrong questions to the right/wrong people – "Would you prefer the Affordable Healthcare Act or the Obamacare Act to be enforced?" Did I already mention that they are the same? And what do guns have to do with it??? Enjoy it here: **http://goo.gl/jSMdjq**

PART
IV

WHAT HAPPENS
OUTSIDE THE
CLASSROOM,
STAYS OUTSIDE THE
CLASSROOM

34

The HBS club fair – sign up for your future friends HERE!

HBS is not only about business cases or parties. It's also a great place to build social relationships with a magnitude of people from different backgrounds and cultures. HBS Clubs were initiated as a fun way for students with similar interests to meet and to enjoy themselves. Today, there are a total of 76 student clubs at HBS for a MBA student body of about 1800.

At the start of the new academic year, all of these clubs unite in the HBS sports center, where the basketball courts are transformed into a giant student club fair. This can be best described as a speed-dating session between students and clubs. Some of the clubs are industry oriented, others focus on regional/racial groups, while the rest of them organize social gatherings or sports activities. Whatever their goal, they all try to stand out at this big event in order to attract as many potential future members as possible.

To do so, some clubs use free gifts (putting my email address down at the 'Venture Capital & Private Equity Club' got me a USB-stick), others just stick to the basics (the 'Francophone Club' advertises with the word 'Bonjour'). And then you have those that rely on humor (the 'Democrats Club', which is free to join, pointed out that the 'Republicans Club' was charging a membership 'tax').

You also have the more colorful clubs such as the 'Euro Club', desperately trying to reposition their brand with the slogan 'not only about parties'… yeah right!' The 'Greater China Club' had a Panda bear greeting all of the visitors to their stand. The 'Rugby Club' was showing off two solid guys wearing very tight shirts…

I signed up to the mailing list of 6-7 clubs. I decided later on where I really wanted to invest my time and money. As most of the clubs charge a yearly membership fee of about $30, the sum of different club memberships can become rather expensive.

Finally, here are some clubs whose existence kind of surprised me:

- The Brew Club (about brewing, drinking or both?)
- Heard on the Street (an acappella band)
- Outdoors Club
- Texas Club (wearing cowboy boots and hats mandatory?)
- Wine & Cuisine society (organizing wine tastings, etc.)

Hmm, no Belgian club at HBS? Well actually, there kind of is one! Some Belgian students in Cambridge started the Belgian club of Harvard and MIT. They created a joint club to increase membership numbers (hey, there are only so many Belgians in the world). As MIT has less stringent conditions for starting a club, the club is incorporated at MIT instead of at Harvard or HBS. The club has 2 presidents – one from each school, and preferably one from each of the language zones in Belgium (French and Dutch). While small with only about 50 members, the Belgian Club was an important part of my time at HBS. During my first year in Boston, I was just a member helping out with organizing activities. The second year I was co-president of the club. I loved it!

I recommend everyone to sign up for at least one club and take on some kind of leadership role. While managing the bigger clubs at HBS (the health-care club, the investment club, etc.) can be a great leadership experience, I very much enjoyed being part of a smaller club where you can really get to know everyone. But again, that's probably very much so linked to my personality type. For those interested, please find the full list of HBS clubs on **http://goo.gl/QdgBhn**

35

HBS talents – more than just brainpower at the HBS Show

What does it take to be famous among the HBS student body? Well, being a star professor at HBS sure helps – think Dean Nohria, Youngme Moon, and Clay Christensen. But it turns out that one doesn't have to be a professor to be well-known among the HBS student body. Tim Butler is one of these non-academics that is well-known at HBS. According to his bio, Tim Butler is the Director of Career Development Programs. In practice, he chairs a couple of sessions during RC year[69] during which he invites students to think about their career choices. He advises all students to 'follow their heart' when making professional choices. His fame has reached such a level that he has joined the star professors in being caricatured during the yearly HBS show. Indeed, once a year, HBS students present a comedy/musical/variety show that is a great parody on life at HBS. And if you ask me, Tim Butler (or at least the student that played his role) was the star of the show of 2014!

There was one particularly brilliant scene starring 'Tim Butler'. Based on the tones of the Ylvis song 'What does the fox say?'[70], Tim Butler was singing his version of the song: 'What does your heart say?' The result was hilarious… and it clearly states the difficulty associated with listening to our hearts[71].

The 2014 HBS show (or should I say musical) had some other great moments. There was the "Our transcripts do not really count" song (to the tune of Total Eclipse of the Heart) and the cleverly made "B-school pressure" hit (to the tune of Queen's Under Pressure).

Besides songs and imitations of professors, the favorite hangouts of HBS students were also featured: the Kong in Harvard Square (great place to dance and to find someone to hook up with), the castle where Newport Ball is held and the omnipresent Aldrich classrooms.

Sure, the show will never make its way to Broadway, but I am very impressed by the cleverness of some of the jokes[72], the great costumes, the scenery used on stage and some of the dancing. It is also fun to see that HBS alums still find their way to Burden Auditorium each year to watch this show that has been around since the mid-90s!

---

69 RC-year – Required Curriculum – the first year at HBS.

70 Find original video here: **http://goo.gl/VjqEaf**

71 Find part of the scene here: **http://goo.gl/Wv8VKN**

72 A lot of the humor comes from great one liners. For example, there's this guy courting a girl during the show: "You really are something special – you are like an intelligent comment in Fin1 (our finance class)!"

Congrats to all students involved in creating the show[73]! Great talents!!! I had a fantastic time. And as for you, dear readers, I invite you to think about what your heart says. Find some excerpts of an earlier show here: **http://goo.gl/xQkKay**

36

The biggest enemy - Yale

Every superhero has its counterpart or enemy – and this is not different for the typical 'superschool'. Harvard and Yale (a 'little school' a bit more than a hundred miles southwest from Boston) have always been sworn enemies. This general rivalry between both schools is reflected in a set of pranks, often linked to the yearly football confrontation between their teams. What is really important about this yearly duel? The tailgate party[74]… and of course all of the SWAG[75]!

I didn't really know what to expect as I headed to my first (American) football game ever. Harvard was about to play Yale at the Harvard Stadium and I was amazed by the hype created around this game between two mediocre college football teams – at least, that is what I was told. Customized SWAG for the game was for sale everywhere, and I have to admit that I wasn't able to resist this strong marketing campaign.

Yale or Harvard take turns hosting the game every year. In 2013, Harvard Stadium was the venue where 30,000 fans gathered for the game. A lot of them were students, most often coming from the massive tailgate party

---

73 As well as those participating in some other dance shows at HBS not mentioned here.
74 According to google.com, a tailgate is a "hinged flap at the back of a truck that can be lowered or removed when loading or unloading the vehicle." In North America, the term tailgate has evolved to also mean to "host or attend a social gathering at which an informal meal is served from the back of a parked vehicle, typically in the parking lot of a sports stadium." In summary, a tailgate is an event prior to a sports game where people barbecue and drink in the parking lot.
75 SWAG, short for "Stuff We All Get", refers to promotional items organizations or companies give to promote their brand(s). Think T-shirts or baseball hats featuring the name of a school. More on SWAG in later chapters.

organized in the hours leading up to the game. However, I was amazed by the diversity of the crowd, as there were a lot of families with kids in the stadium – not just students. Right in front of me, a couple of 70 year olds seemed to be having the time of their lives. This left me wondering what made this game such a big deal. Turns out, it is a tradition that began on November 13, 1875, when the first football game between the schools of Harvard and Yale took place. It seems unclear where the rivalry comes from – it's most likely linked to the fact that both Yale and Harvard are among the nation's most prestigious and oldest universities.

Over the years, the rivalry has led to some clever pranks. When I was at HBS, the Harvard Crimson reported on Harvard students selling T-shirts with the very clear message: "No one ever says: I want to go to Yale when I grow up." My all-time favorite prank was the stunt conceived and coordinated by two Yale students in the Class of 2005. With the help of 20 classmates, disguised as the "Harvard Pep Squad," the perpetrators handed white and crimson placards to fans in the central area of the Harvard side of the stadium. The group told the crowd that by lifting the placards they would spell "GO HARVARD." In reality, the placards spelled: "WE SUCK"[76].

As for the game itself, Harvard won – of course! It took me two quarters to understand the rules of American football. Moreover, I was astonished by the slow pace of the game. It seems there are more breaks and timeouts than actual playing minutes, turning the 4 * 15 minute game into an almost 4 hour contest. I need more action I guess…

I'll just stick to soccer…

37

The SA Cup – play for fun and/or to win

The SA Cup (short for the Student Association Cup) is so much more than an athletic competition between the sections. The Student Asso-

---

ciation describes it as "the epitome of athletic success at HBS." They refer to it as a competition between RC and EC sections in a variety of team and individual sports with the winner gaining a cup and lifelong bragging rights.

The SA Cup sports include flag football[77], indoor soccer, volleyball, squash, racquetball, tennis, dodgeball, capture the flag, a 10K running race and finally, the all-important section Olympics[78] in the spring. Points can also be earned in other ways – performing well at the weekly trivia hosted in Spangler cafeteria can score a section a lot of points too.

At the end of the day, the huge difference in points earned between sections reveals more than just a genuine difference in athletic fitness between them; it also indicates part of the culture in a section. Some sections take section pride more seriously than others. One section might 'staff' its basketball team with its star players only, while a competing section might focus more on inclusion than on performance. I have seen sections that had one or two players having 50% or more ball possession during a game compared to teams sharing the joy amongst the players.

The SA Cup is what you want to make of it as a section. For some, the slogan 'participating is more important than winning' is the main focus, others tend to be a bit more competitive about it all. But competition is fierce and most students love winning. After all, it's HBS!

I participated in a couple of events for the SA Cup. I gained the most points for my section in the one thing I am relatively good at – table tennis. Every week or so I would go for a practice session with some of my section mates. This would both be for fun… AND to prepare for the yearly table tennis competition at HBS organized across sections in the gym hall building named Shad. The event is organized by members of the Student Association. And truth be told, they did a fantastic job. They managed the events and provided updates on points scored for the section throughout the SA Cup.

---

77 I didn't know about this sport. It is a variant of football where players don't tackle one another. Instead, they stop each other's progress on the field by pulling a piece of cloth stuck to the outside of their pants on a special belt.

78 The section Olympics feature traditional Olympic disciplines such as 'eat as much hot dogs as possible in 10 minutes' and carrying an egg on a spoon. Find out how students prepare for the section Olympics here: **http://goo.gl/u8ba1W**

At the end of the day, my section ended up winning the SA Cup! And while I only made a small contribution with points earned from my table tennis performance (compared to some big wins we had in basketball and flag football for instance), I am happy to hereby fully exert my lifelong bragging rights on the win. Go Section C!

38

Breakfast with the Dean – Starbucks is coming to town!?!

A couple of times a year, students have the opportunity to meet Dean Nohria over breakfast. As demand outweighs supply for breakfast spots, the HBS administration cleverly uses a lottery to assign spots to those who signed up for the breakfast. I was one of the lucky ones who got in!

The breakfast took place at Kresge building, just days before they started to tear it down to replace it with a new building[79]. It was thus Dean Nohria's last breakfast in this building, and I was lucky enough to join him for it, along with five other HBS MBAs.

I didn't know all that much about Dean Nohria prior to breakfast. I knew he used to be part of the teaching staff at HBS. I knew that he was the first Dean in quite some time at HBS that actually lives on campus (yes, there is a house for the Dean of HBS on campus). And my interactions with him had been limited to attending a couple of his presentations to the entire HBS student body. To be honest, I hadn't been that impressed by what I had seen from him till then.

Little did I know that the breakfast would totally change my view on him. In this small group discussion with students, he came across as an exceptionally smart and witty man. It was the way he answered our questions (he is extremely well-spoken) and the confidence with which he answered them (he has the habit of leaning forward when answering a tough ques-

---

79 I always wondered how that worked from a naming point of view. Kresge, who donated the money for that building, will lose his legacy on campus overnight? Poor guy!?!

tion) that made me change my mind about him. He also seemed to have a brain that worked faster than the speed of light. What surprised me most is that these qualities didn't come across in the same way when addressing larger crowds. Or maybe I was the one not paying enough attention.

While Dean Nohria was open to any form of feedback or questions during breakfast, I found most of the chat to be very neutral. A lot of questions were linked to diversity at HBS and the role of women at HBS (we had just celebrated the 50 year anniversary of women being admitted to HBS). Other questions were related to the FIELD program (more on that later). When we ran out of questions, Dean Nohria discussed random things such as the fact that the new Kresge building might host an on-campus Starbucks (beats the 10 minute walk to Harvard Square for the nearest Starbucks)!

As I was eating my complementary cereal sponsored by HBS, some interesting questions pop up in my head. How will HBS address the peer pressure leading to some of the students living absurdly expensive lifestyles[80] funded by increasing amounts of personal debt? What role does HBS intend to play in the changing role of business in the world, with an increased focus on social responsibility? Should HBS become more international and not only focus on its Cambridge campus? For some reason, I didn't feel compelled to ask these questions during breakfast. Was it the politically correct atmosphere that was hanging in the air? Was I just tired because of the early morning wakeup? I am not sure – all I know is that I wish I could have another breakfast with him and ask the real questions. I might not have found out about the soon-to-be Starbucks on campus, it would however have been a much more enriching conversation with this smart and witty man.

On a final note, I was shocked by the fact that only 6 out of 8 selected students showed up that morning for breakfast. I guess the 7AM starting time of the breakfast had something to do with that, but then again, don't sign up for it if you can't get out of bed. This is something that has often bothered me at HBS: students' inability to actually live up to commitments made. and as such deprive others of the opportunity to have breakfast with

---

80 More on this in the "Giving HBS a Bad Name" Chapter.

the Dean. Maybe one of my questions to Dean Nohria should have been how he felt about those unexcused absences and what it meant to him...

39

HBS breaks – work hard and/or play hard

The HBS MBA is of a full-time 2-year program – but full-time doesn't mean there is no time for play. The 2 years spent getting an MBA degree include a couple of breaks. To some, the breaks are more important than the actual time spent in the classroom. Find an overview of the 3 types of breaks at HBS and their specificities below.

First, there are the short holiday breaks. They include a couple of days off for Thanksgiving[81] in November and a full week off in March for Spring Break. Of course, the end of December is reserved for family and friends, with courses at HBS typically ending around December 10th and exams finishing by December 20th.

Second, there are two winter breaks, which tend to be filled in a variety of ways. The first winter break during RC year is monopolized by the FIELD2 program (read more on FIELD2 later) and recruiting for summer. The second one in EC year is a real break for most students, with each student filling this time in very different ways. One option is to go on holiday and travel.

Most students see travel as a key priority during their time in school, as most of them will have very intense professional lives going forward – hence the need to fully optimize the less condensed time in school. And while I also explored different continents during my time at HBS, I was also amazed by the number of fantastic places to visit within the U.S. As an international student, it was the ideal occasion to discover a lot of the interesting cities and sights the U.S. had to offer (Los Angeles, San Francisco, Las Vegas, New York, Austin etc.).

---

81 Note that HBS staff invite international students to join them for their family Thanksgiving meals.

Travel plans can be organized personally, or through a trek organized by one of the HBS clubs. And since there are students from all over the world at HBS, these treks can literally take you places. I remember treks being organized in Israel (oversubscribed), Egypt and Saudi Arabia. Or for those not so interested in the Middle East, there was the very successful Japan trek! Other students get to see different parts of the world while on a professional assignment, some kind of micro-internship with a company or getting work done for an employer-to-be. Finally, there are those that sign up for the HBS IXP (immersion experience program).

An IXP is an elective course offered as part of the 2nd year program at HBS. It consists of a couple of preparatory courses during the first term and then a +/- 10-day trip to the selected country, where students will typically work on consultancy projects. During my time at HBS, students were able to sign up for IXPs in China and Japan. It seems the offering of IXPs has gone downhill in recent years though, as it used to include more exotic destinations such as UAE, India, and Rwanda. I believe IXPs can be considered the pioneer of the FIELD2 program, which is currently part of the first year at HBS. Some important differences between both programs are that FIELD2 is mandatory compared to IXP, and that the full cost of the FIELD2 program is paid for by HBS and its generous sponsors.[82] IXP programs require a contribution of the students – plan to spend up to $3500 for the Japan IXP[83].

Third, there is the 3-month-long summer break. Again, travel and treks are popular options with students, but most time is spent on either internships or working on start-ups. It is a great time to prepare for one's future career and/or to explore industries and cultures that one would otherwise never experience. My summer was intense, with two internships in two different industries on two different continents (more on internships later). And as I worked all summer long, I decided to fully devote my winter break to holidays and travel…on yet a third continent.

---

82 This may have changed in recent years.
83 Find an infomercial of HBS on IXP here: **http://goo.gl/fNdIUC**

40

The HBS tag (summer) cloud – I know what HBS students did last summer

I had the best of times during my HBS summer between the first and second year of my MBA program. Although I worked non-stop during the three-month break, I enjoyed every second of it – working partially in Europe and in Asia. I will elaborate on my personal internship summer experiences later in this book, but I wondered how representative my summer was of what a typical HBS summer looks like. So before giving a full report of my summer, here's an overview of how my fellow section mates spent their time.

I consolidated all of the update emails I received from them. These were not just random emails – rather they were part of a relatively young tradition at HBS: the 92 days of summer. Each of my 92 section mates was assigned a date at the beginning of summer. On that date, each of us was to send an email to the whole section to share our summer experiences.

It was a real pleasure to read those emails. Some of them were short and to the point. Others were a detailed report of activities. And then there were those I considered beautiful pieces of writing and storytelling.

To summarize my section mates' summers, I decided to compile these emails into one document and have it summarized by a tagcloud.[84]

Let's have a closer look at the 'HBS Summer Tag' awards:
Overall winner: WORK
… which I guess makes a lot of sense…
Best adverb: REALLY
… summer experiences must have been REALLY intense…
Commercial award: NIKE
… the most-tagged brand name in our tag cloud… I guess one could call this clever use of social media…

---

84 Find the HBS summer tagcloud here: **http://goo.gl/8fU9Uu**

Best gender award: GUYS

... GUYS was used more than the word GALS... hmmmm...

Geography award: ISRAEL

... a lot of tags for Israel... well, I did notice from the emails that the Israel trek was a huge success!!!

Most unexplainable word: DON ... ??? ...

Well, I hope this gives you an idea of what the HBS summer looks like... three valuable months between our first and second year at HBS... After summer, it was time to start counting down to the start of the second year at HBS after a REALLY amazing summer with a lot of WORK and beautiful... eh ... GUYS...!?!

41

The Harvard Innovation Lab – Palo Alto on the East Coast

The Harvard Innovation Lab (or i-Lab) first opened its doors in 2011. The i-Lab is Harvard's attempt to bring more (potential) entrepreneurs to the school. Stanford is directly associated with the dynamic and entrepreneurial Palo Alto. With entrepreneurship becoming a growing area of interest for students, Harvard had to find a way to support those aspirations.

While the i-Lab is part of the HBS campus, it is supposed to be a meeting place for all different Harvard faculties. In reality, due to its distance from the rest of the schools (those 'over-the-river'), one sees mainly HBS students spending their time in the i-Lab workplace. And students can do so comfortably, while enjoying free drinks and snacks on the house.

But more than a free treat, the i-Lab offers courses, presentations and trainings to help those interested in entrepreneurship to further develop their skills. I was impressed by some of the fairs organized at the i-Lab, where young entrepreneurs or small companies would look for talent ready to take a professional risk by joining them. Some companies have a live demonstration of their products under development, while others shared their business model.

More than offering a space to work and to meet, the i-Lab also tries to support entrepreneurs through different initiatives. One of them is the Venture Incubation Program (VIP), which aims to provide entrepreneurial students with professional guidance over a 12-week period. They also deliver all kinds of courses and workshops on a variety of topics that could be helpful for aspiring entrepreneurs. And last but not least, they host different competitions (some driven by the school, others sponsored by venture capital or similar firms) to challenge students to come up with innovative ideas that could result in making the business a reality. The question remains however, if an entrepreneurial environment is one that can be created artificially.

Right after my last exam at HBS, I took a trip to the west coast of the U.S. and visited the Stanford campus. The setting is very different from HBS – everything seems to happen outside (the weather, remember?) and the atmosphere just feels much more relaxed. When talking to students, it's all about entrepreneurship, the facilities offered by the school and the surrounding 'breeding area' to support it[85]. This includes sponsored legal support from law firms (as they hope to have some of these companies turn into the next Google – as such courting new potential big clients), proactive venture capital firms supporting small student endeavors, and the thousands of already present start-ups in the vicinity that are actively recruiting talented young professionals for start-up jobs.

After what I saw in the San Francisco area, I realized that Boston still has a long way to go to make it to that level. And it left me wondering if the artificially and rigidly orchestrated environment of the i-Lab could drive that change. Nonetheless, I admire HBS's efforts to provide students with the tools to develop their plans. Moreover, the i-Lab is still very young – the future might prove me wrong.

MIT (the school right next door to Harvard in Cambridge) might be an example for Harvard to follow. A couple of decades ago, they founded the

---

85 Stanford even lets students experiment with self-driving trash cans in the cafeteria. I use the word 'experiment' on purpose – as that thing bumped into me twice!

MIT Media Lab. The Lab's mission is to "actively promote a unique, anti-disciplinary culture" and create "disruptive technologies that happen at the edges." Sounds cool, right? I have visited the Media Lab on multiple occasions, and had friends working there (or should I say living there?). It is a pretty magical place to visit, and it feels like a much less constrained place than the i-Lab. I also believe location matters. While the Media Lab is located in the middle of the MIT campus, the i-Lab is a bit out of the way for most students. It is at the far end of the HBS campus and not connected to the underground tunnel network at HBS (hence students need to brave the harsh winter to reach the building), which is a solid 20 minute walk from most of the other Harvard faculties. The location could be less problematic in the near future, as I was told that Harvard's engineering school will open a new campus right across the street from the i-Lab.

I personally only frequented the i-Lab[86] on a couple of occasions. I didn't really like its artificial environment and had a hard time concentrating on work with people playing a soccer game on the Xbox next to me. But then again, I might not have an entrepreneurial mindset. Hence, I would still recommend aspiring entrepreneurs to check out the i-Lab and all they have to offer. And if the workspace is not what makes you tick, you can try their matchmaking services for entrepreneurs online! Enjoy the speed-dating at **http://goo.gl/0q2eFM**

86 Find some more info on the i-Lab here:
http://goo.gl/SfM9ky   **http://goo.gl/ZgqPci**   **http://goo.gl/Zl7sZj**

PART V

V

GIVING HBS A BAD NAME

42

Ethics at HBS – let's not repeat the same mistakes twice

HBS MBAs (as well as some of the MBAs of other schools and many, many non-MBAs) have been involved in some of the most important financial scandals of the last decades. People like Jeffrey Skilling (former CEO of Enron), Kirk Shelton (former vice chairman of Cendant Corp) and Alan Bond (former pension fund manager) are all Harvard MBAs, but just the three of them combined have accumulated sentences of more than 40 years of jail time for fraud.

While non-MBAs also commit white collar crimes, the public perception is that a lot of top-school MBAs are to blame for some of the fraudulent actions that have impacted many. This perception seems to persist, as actress Mindy Kaling proved during her commencement speech at Harvard Law School, saying jokingly to the graduating law students that "you are entering a profession where, no matter what the crime, you have to defend the alleged perpetrator. Across the campus, Harvard Business School graduates are receiving diplomas, and you will have to defend them – for insider trading or narcotics, or maybe both if Wolf of Wall Street is to be believed."[87]

HBS has taken a strong stance on the importance of ethics in business. First of all, all HBS MBAs are enrolled in two courses focusing on human behavior and ethics in business – LEAD (Leadership and organizational behavior) and LCA (Leadership and Corporate Accountability). The importance of ethics is also stressed in other classes. During the first-year FRC class (Financial Reporting and Control, the HBS version of an accounting class), we had a case called 'Letter from Prison'[88]. The case is about Stephen Richards, the former global head of sales at Computer Associates, Inc. (CA), who is serving a 7-year prison sentence for financial fraud.

87 Find her full speech here: **http://goo.gl/P3gWDu** (fast forward to minute 14 for the quote)
88 Soltes, Eugene F. "A Letter from Prison." Harvard Business School Case 110-045, December 2009. (Revised March 2011)

In the case, Richards responds to a number of questions about managerial responsibility and the manipulation of financial performance in a letter written to a graduate student. It provides interesting insights in how a condemned man reflects on his behavior.

Have times changed? Or not? The future will tell. At one point, I was very surprised to see banners hanging around campus from a HBS professor with the text: "You've got to break the rules. You've got to try and come up with a different way of doing things." Nothing all too surprising... albeit that this came from a professor in accounting!?! Lesson not learned?[89]

Not only HBS, but also students themselves are trying to turn the tide. The MBA oath initiative[90], started in 2009 by a couple of students, seems a good start. Its goal is to get students to commit to being "MBAs who aim to lead in the interests of the greater good and who have committed to living out the principles articulated in the oath" – it is a kind of Hippocratic oath for MBAs. The future will tell how important initiatives like this are.

43

Being part of HBS – respecting the norms

Being admitted to HBS is a privilege – at the same time, being associated with the HBS brand also comes with the responsibility of maintaining the reputation of HBS. HBS has a set of community values that apply to all students and staff or anyone linked to HBS – they are as follows:

- Respect for the rights, differences, and dignity of others
- Honesty and integrity in dealing with all members of the community
- Accountability for personal behavior

---

89 Of course, this comment was taken out of context. The professor in question didn't have the intention to promote illegal activities. Still, I found it a daring statement to make by an accounting professor at a moment in time where a lot of fraudulent cases had just come to light...

90 Find out more here: **http://goo.gl/l8gzBI** and here: **http://goo.gl/whZ26A**

90a

90b

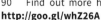

HBS hold students accountable for upholding its norms and values. Different sessions are organized in the respective class sections for students to think about section norms – how do students in a section want to interact with one another in the next two years? HBS gives the sections a lot of freedom to define those norms. The norms are discussed in class (often facilitated by students of the section), written down and displayed in the classroom.

I see a lot of value having these sessions, though I believe it is nearly impossible to have a fruitful discussion about values in a group of nearly one hundred people. By default, the conversation will be led by about ten individuals with strong views or opinions, which maybe is not a bad thing, but might lead to a set of values that is not reflective of everyone's views in the section. Also, most norms and values end up aligned to those of American culture and society[91]. Alternatively, having a small but representative group of people (that has gotten to know the section as a whole in the first few weeks of school) work on a set of values first, then present them to the class for discussion might be a better way of working.

For completeness, please note that besides the section values, HBS also has a school honor code. With students being allowed to take exams from home, it is important for students to comply with this honor code. The HBS administration relies on the honor code to prevent cheating or unauthorized collaboration between students on exams. Find more info on HBS values and honor code here: **http://goo.gl/53orhd**

44

Party tickets shortage – let's make a profit then?

Some of the HBS parties are big hits and tickets sell out within the first hour. These party tickets seem to be as valuable as concert-tickets for [FILL NAME OF CURRENT HOT BAND HERE]. So here is a question: should busi-

---

91 Americans are by far the most represented nationality in a section – moreover, Americans tend to be the most outspoken ones in class.

ness students stay truthful to their belief in the free market system and raise prices for HBS parties on the secondary market?

Well, one guy that shall remain anonymous tried to make a profit reselling his tickets on a HBS-group on Facebook the day before the [FILL NAME OF PARTY WHERE ONE HAS TO BE]-party. The face value per ticket was $40 – he offered his ticket for sale at a 150% markup. Part of the HBS-crowd started complaining about his practices. He reacted defensively, saying that we live in a capitalist society. Most disagreed with his views, some agreed. I don't know if he managed to sell his tickets in the end, and at what price, but it did show some of the capitalistic mindset at HBS, as well as the divergence of views around it.

Is HBS all about making money? Should the free market principle be the one and only guiding principal? Or was this just a meaningless intermezzo between parties?

45

Some rumors on "Section X"...and The Black & White society

In 2013, the New York Times (NYT) published a set of articles on HBS. One of the articles discussed the problem of class divide at HBS[92]. Indeed, with HBS struggling to get its bad image off its back in relation to the gender divide, there seems to be an even bigger divide that is threatening an equal experience at HBS nowadays – the socioeconomic class divide.

Students are under social pressure to spend more and more money to keep up with a bustling social life at HBS. I once told my section mates that I would not attend a school-wide event as I found it too expensive for my partner and I. The next day, I was approached by two section-mates from the section leadership, telling me that they wanted to 'help me out financially' and pay for part of the ticket so we could participate. The money would come from the section budget, paid for by the section dues.

92 Find the article here: **http://goo.gl/1eq8iG**

I didn't know how to respond to this gesture. On one hand, I believe they were trying to do the right thing. On the other hand, I felt bad being treated like a 'poor guy', having to be offered a subsidized meal. I eventually thanked them for the offer, telling them I would rather spend my dollars on something else at that moment. The class divide at HBS can thus be seen to different extents. I believe there are three groups: those who can, those who borrow, and those who don't care. The first group worked in top-earning jobs before or came from family money – money is never an issue when looking at fun things to do. The second group sees money as an issue, but they decided to make the most of their time at HBS and just take out another loan for their studies that trip to Peru. And then there are those who just don't care and attend what they want.

The article in the NYT referred to the existence of a section X – a secret society of people from the first group who can afford to fly to say Hong Kong for the weekend, followed by a trip to Iceland the next week. I don't know about the existence of such a group. I do know that some people indeed come from (a lot of) money and can easily do these things. But then again, in everyday life, some people fly economy and others fly business class – what's the difference? If the people who are able to go on such a spending spree like to spend time together doing crazy things spending money – why not?

The Harbus[93] published an interesting reaction to the NYT article[94], stating more or less what I described above. They also refer to the exclusive Black and White party hosted only for the 'Finest Individuals' – or at least the 300 finest HBS students. This is an invite-only party. If you are not on the list, you don't get in. And nobody is entirely sure what it takes to be on that list. Fact is, the Black and White party is an important event for some, and is totally meaningless for others. The former group of people see it as a key achievement to be invited to that party, the latter couldn't care less.

I was not invited to this party – and I didn't quite expect to be invited either. I believe anyone organizing a party or any kind of event has the liberty to invite who they want, whether it is an event at HBS or in a different

93 Harbus is the HBS student newspaper.
94 Find the Harbus article here: **http://goo.gl/SVjUPf**

context. What makes this specific party controversial, is that it has become a tradition –something that former attendees can brag about. But I frankly don't care. If that's what makes people happy, so be it. I too organized parties. One of them was in my apartment, which can accommodate about 40 to 50 people. Inviting my whole section was simply put, impossible, so should I feel bad about only inviting those that I care most about? The difference being that for Section X or the Black & White Society, the sole consideration is class divide.

Class divide is something that is part of the society we live in. At HBS, this divide might be even more visible, as it is home to some from modest backgrounds and some super-rich. I don't believe it is a HBS problem. It is a societal problem which is exacerbated at elite schools like HBS.

46

HBS commitment – sign up now / decide later

There are different types of students at HBS. There are those who put a lot of effort into organizing amazing activities. Then there are those that are really good at signing up for tons of great things. And finally, there are those who are excellent at showing up for great activities. Unfortunately, the second group and the third group of students only partially overlap, often leaving the students from the first group with a lot of headaches.

Indeed, one of my big frustrations at HBS was the low level of commitment. HBS students struggle to keep firm to earlier promises to attend events – what if something better shows up? So here is James, organizing a great entrepreneurial trek in Boston (more on that later), visiting a set of young successful companies in the region. James organized a full-day program and planned visits at set times during the day with the entrepreneurs. He can take 12 students on the trip. Sign-up is free. But James knows that some students will not show up at the last minute, so everyone who wants to sign up has to write him a check for $200. If they show up on the day of the entrepreneurial trek, he rips the check. Those who fail to show up will lose $200. Even then, two MBA students didn't show up for the trek. What does it take for HBS students to commit?

PART

VI

THE REMARKABLE
HBS ASSETS

47

The HBS facilities – not the average cafeteria and gym[95]

The most symbolic HBS fixed asset is without a doubt Baker Library, which is very recognizable thanks to its tall white columns and bell tower on top. Upon entering the building, students find themselves in quite a luxurious environment with leather seats and a dozen flat screens featuring CNN and business TV channels. For low tech people, it is the place to find fresh copies of all kinds of international (business) newspapers. While spacious and located in the center of the campus, the library is not a place where one sees many students. I guess the digital age is to blame.

Spangler cafeteria is a far better place for student spotting than the library. Spangler houses two different restaurants that offer sandwiches, prepared food ranging from sushi to pasta and a pretty impressive salad bar. I was surprised to find that Spangler, being a student cafeteria, has its own reviews on Yelp[96]. I rated Spangler four stars and strongly recommend the sushi, which is made fresh right there in front of you!

Shad is where most of the sweating is going on at HBS. The Shad building hosts a gym, different sets of courts (be it for tennis, squash, basketball, volleyball or soccer), an indoor running track and much, much more. Shad also offers some less sweaty entertainment; such as dance classes. I learned my first salsa moves in Shad!

Aldrich, right in front of the Spangler building, is the place where most of the teaching magic happens. It has a dozen U-shaped classrooms and some alcoves where students can prepare for class and work together in small groups. The alcoves are particularly useful, as I find HBS sometimes lacks places for students to collaborate. Moreover, they are shaped in a semi-circle, allowing students to easily share information. On the downside, the alcoves tend to get really cold in summer (too much aircon) and very hot in winter (too much heating).

---

95 Find a map of the HBS campus here: **http://goo.gl/8VKAVV**
96 Find reviews here: **http://goo.gl/0KZNAt**

95

96

And then there are some monstrosities on the HBS campus. The Rock center is an ugly concrete square located between stylish Spangler and Aldrich. But the real monster in my opinion is the student housing building called One Western Ave (OWA). OWA is supposed to look like a bridge, but is in reality a very inconvenient, confusing and weird-looking building. This is in contrast to other older student housing buildings at HBS, which are nicely designed and often have classy common rooms for students to hang out. They tend to be equipped with pianos and (again) leather seats.

Perhaps some of the design disasters of the Rock Center and OWA have led HBS to take less risks when adding new buildings to the campus recently. There is no safer bet than a building with glass walls nowadays, as they did with the newly erected Tata building. In the spring of 2014, HBS proudly opened this latest building to the public. The Tata building (buildings are traditionally named after one of its biggest donors – the Tata Trust donated $50m for the construction of the building) will mainly be dedicated to executive education. This is clearly expressed through its very corporate design with tons of glass and shiny bright walls. It's the same type of building used in a Tata Nano car commercial, in which the car literally drives onto the building to avoid traffic[97]. It is the first building in that style on the HBS campus. While the building looks nice, it lacks character, which I believe to be a missed opportunity. One doesn't get a $50m donation every year to invest in the campus. In my view, HBS could have built something more daring... even if there's always the risk that some will perceive it as yet another monstrosity on campus.

HBS also caters to young families with kids. There is a full-blown daycare on campus and one can often see the 'young ones' stroll around campus (all holding tight to a rope that links them together). And before I forget, there is this random turkey that seems to loiter around Cambridge and the Harvard campus. I have seen it many times – not sure if it can be considered a Harvard asset or not. As far as I know, it survived last Thanksgiving.

---

97 Watch it at **http://goo.gl/5NHuST**

48

Overpriced sushi and Crimson cash to pay for it!

Working hard in class leaves the average student very hungry. Luckily, HBS has an excellent food court in the Spangler building, offering all kinds of food. The food is surprisingly good for a cafeteria, and the selection is diverse – proof of that is my Dad's comment after I dropped my parents off in the cafeteria for breakfast when they visited: "I could eat here every day!" (and my Dad's a chef, remember?!?). There are healthy options (I highly recommend the salad bar and the excellent sushi counter), and then there are the less healthy options (pizza and cookies anyone?). Finally, there are the homemade muffins, as advertised by HBS[98]!

For HBS students, alternative food options are very limited. Some food trucks pull up nearby on student demand, but service tends to be slow and the menu is usually limited. Students could walk to say Harvard Square for lunch, but the cold weather most of the year and the 10-minute walk makes it a tough trip between classes.

So while the food and service at Spangler are great, Spangler's monopolistic advantage can be tough on students' wallets. Simple things like a cup of soup or a small pack of sushi are way overpriced. Comparing the prices at the HBS food court to that of the nearby MIT food court, there seems to be a 20 to 30% inflation. Even drinks tend to be expensive, with a Coke going at a 40% mark-up. HBS can do so with very little competition close by.

It's not always straightforward to keep track of spending in the HBS cafeterias. Apart from Spangler, there are smaller food courts located in Aldrich and the i-Lab, where one is often tempted to stop for a quick bite. Moreover, the whole campus accepts Crimson cash, a form of stored value on one's student card. A quick swipe at the register and 'hop' – payment done.

Crimson cash can also be used in all vending machines around campus. Reloads can be done online or even through a convenient Campus cash

 98 Watch a video on the muffins made-at-HBS by their overnight baker here: **http://goo.gl/QhHbK5**

app. But then again, could we really expect anything less from a leading business school?

49

The Harbus – the one source of information for all that's crucial in (campus) life

I refer on several occasions to the Harbus throughout this book. According to their website harbus.org, the Harbus is "a self-funded, student-run, non-profit organization and publisher of The Harbus newspaper." The Harbus newspaper is distributed free on the HBS campus and has a strong online presence as well. Find more information and interesting articles on **http://goo.gl/Tn5yTZ**

The Harbus is an indispensable / funny / intellectual / informative / creative source of news on life at HBS. It is made by students for students – hence the articles often depict a very accurate and informative view of life on campus. Moreover, most columns in the Harbus are opinionated. Just as in the magazine The Economist, the writers take a stand on a certain issue or news item. They share their opinion on trending topics such as the socioeconomic class divide at Harvard Business School, or a controversial decision of the HBS administration. I love it!

The one Harbus edition that stands out though is on a much lighter subject – the 'HBS most eligible' (bachelors and bachelorettes) election contest. I loved reading the profiles of the 'chosen ones'. The questions & answers segment includes:

- Any deal breakers? When he forgets my name halfway into the date
- Any deal breakers? Manorexia
- Finish this sentence: Love is…a low marginal tax rate
- Finish this sentence: Love is…letting me watch football all weekend
- What is your best attribute? I can divide by zero
- What are you looking for in a prospective romantic partner? Positive cash flow

- What is your pre-date ritual? Yodeling in my Lederhosen. Like all Austrians.

They are joking, right? Find the full report at
http://goo.gl/H5pgvG

50

The Harvard Crimson

Ah, the Harvard Crimson. While the more 'local' Harbus newspaper focuses on life at HBS and is published weekly, the Harvard Crimson is our daily friend on weekdays covering the whole Harvard society. And it has to be said, the Harvard Crimson includes an impressive mix of serious topics and less intellectual ones. The Harvard Crimson will update us about the latest financial investment made by the Harvard fund, but also the score of the Harvard-Yale football game. They will focus on a strike in a nearby Cambridge hotel, and will discuss the different candidates for the upcoming undergraduate student council elections. More importantly, they will also inform us that a smashing 65% of freshmen at Harvard are virgins and that alum have tons of money to spend on Harvard. What's not to like about the Harvard Crimson?[99]

Like Harbus, the Harvard Crimson is distributed free. Most students pick it up from one of the holders at the entrance of Aldrich, and so did I. Contrary to the Harbus, which I would pick up every week when a fresh edition was published, I would only take a fresh copy of the Crimson depending on its headline. The Crimson has a much more professional look and feel than the Harbus, but its content is often of less interest to me than the Harbus, hence my habit of scanning the headline prior to grabbing it. And yes, the Crimson also has a digital version. Call me old fashioned, but nothing beats reading off a crumbled piece of recycled paper in the minutes before and between classes. Thanks for still having a print copy for the local dinosaurs (that's me!), guys!

---

99 Find out more at **http://goo.gl/HBQajT**

51

The HBS Nobel prize winning algorithm – how to impress the machine, not the humans...

One of the basic assumptions in economics is that everything is based on the simple relationship between supply and demand. If demand for a service or a good exceeds supply, prices will go up (think expensive airplane tickets around Thanksgiving or Christmas) and vice versa (think a midweek flight at 11AM). But how do you match supply and demand when basic economics do not work – i.e. when you cannot put a price to it (think a really great course at HBS for which there are only 90 seats available with 900 students who want to sign up for it)? Well, one could run a lottery for those interested in the good or service, reward people based on merit, or use math and statistics to determine who gets what. And for two of its most scarce resources, the latter is exactly what HBS ended up doing. Meet the HBS algorithm for the allocation of the elective courses and FIELD2[100] destinations.

It is interesting how the allocation of these scarce resources at HBS is fully left to a machine running an algorithm, while the whole process of getting accepted to HBS, also a scarce resource, seems completely dependent on humans. A straight 800 GMAT score alone is not a criteria for acceptance. Nor will perfect essays or grades do the trick. Not something a computer can decide on. However, once accepted at HBS, it seems that HBS considers its students a bunch of equals. A top-notch academic performance in your first year at HBS will not get you VIP treatment for the course selection for your second year. Perhaps HBS did not want to create additional competition between students in that field. Or do they just want to avoid the additional headache of having to screen the students over and over again?

Then again, HBS does not rely on just any random allocation method either for their scarce resources. They rely on a Nobel-prize winning algorithm developed by Alvin Roth, the Gund Professor of Economics and Business Administration Emeritus at Harvard University. And HBS does not

---

100 Read up more on FIELD2 later – as part of FIELD2, HBS students are sent to a developing country as consultants on a project for a local company.

expect you to be bluffed by using the algorithm of a world-famous professor – they even go as far as taking students through a simulation exercise
in class to demonstrate the value of it! In the case "Chances are…"[101] HBS
'advertises' the method it uses for course selection in comparison to the
system used by Kellogg (another highly ranked U.S. business school). The
case illustrates how students can influence the decision on which elective
courses they are selected for. HBS students can only rank their preferred
courses from 1 to x, while the Kellogg system requires students to allocate
points to a course as a proxy for how badly they want it. Of course, each
student is allocated a limited and equal amount of points.

Prior to the class case discussion, students access an online simulation
tool in which they attempt to optimize their preferred choice of classes
using both systems. During class, the results of the simulation, i.e. which
classes they got assigned to, are shared with students. Students could then
see which system gave them the best result. When the professor asked for
a show of hands on which system provided the best results, the vast majority responded that the HBS algorithm gave them their preferred outcome.
I admit being somewhat surprised by this. The Kellogg system, which gives
the highest level of input and control to students, did not lead to an optimal
allocation of resources. The HBS allocation, based on a simple ranking of
preference, did.

The same applies for the allocation of FIELD2 destinations. Again, HBS
relies on Professor Roth's algorithm to allocate the limited amount of precious FIELD2 destinations. As part of FIELD2, all first year students at HBS
get to work on a project in a developing country. Different destinations are
offered to students – and some have a supply/demand mismatch that cannot be solved by a pricing mechanism, and thus the need for the algorithm.
My input was limited to ranking the available countries from 1 to 10[102]. But
how does this algorithm work exactly? Let's take the example of the FIELD2
allocation of preferred destinations. The algorithm would assign a random
number from 1 to 900 to all students. The algorithm will then start with the

---

101   Hanna Halaburda and Aldo Sesia. "Chances Are? Course Selection at HBS and at
Kellogg." HBS Case (711-449) and Teaching Note
102   Find my personal input to the FIELD2 algorithm here:
http://goo.gl/t16UId – and yes, the algorithm got me what I wanted.

student who got assigned #1 and will give him/her his/her first choice. Then the student with #2 will receive his/her first choice, etc. – the algorithm will do so for all 900 students and give them their first choice wherever possible. After the first round ending with student #900, the algorithm will now start from this student and allocate their top choice (in case they have not been allocated a choice yet). Next up is the student with #899, etc. During each iteration, the system will try to give the student their top choice. If not available anymore, it will skip to the next student. The algorithm keeps on moving back and forth until all students have been assigned a spot.

As with the elective course selection, all students can do here is rank their preferred countries from 1 to 10, and even then it was a tough choice. One can choose between 10 countries over five continents, not that obvious of a choice! So here's my personal thought process. First, I wanted to experience a country I hadn't visited before. Hence, Turkey, Malaysia and China were at the end of the list. Second, I excluded countries I would likely visit for holiday one day – hence the low rank for Argentina, South Africa and Vietnam (I did visit two of those places as a tourist later!). To be honest, I initially had Brazil on this list as well, but I felt some kind of special attraction to Brazil (dreams of Rio and Sao Paolo) during this exercise, hence I kept it on my shortlist.

So now Brazil, Chile, India and Ghana were the remaining contenders. I was tempted by Brazil and Chile, but realized that Ghana would be a once-in-a-lifetime experience. I have to admit it was a bit of a challenging choice, as it was difficult to imagine what to expect from conducting business in Ghana. But with a little push from my adventurous girlfriend, Ghana it would be. And then I ended up being indifferent between Brazil and Chile.

At the end of the day, I was a fan of Professor Roth's algorithm, as it gave me my adventurous top choice Ghana (although that was one of the destinations with fewer number of spots available). Thanks Professor Roth! Though it has to be said – I felt less enthusiastic about his algorithm when I saw the outcome of the EC course selection (see next chapter).

52

The HBS electives' wheel of fortune...

In RC year, all students get the same ten classes. They focus on the basics of business, with courses in finance and accounting, marketing and supply chain, leadership and ethics, strategy and macro-economics. However, HBS's second year (the EC year) allows students to select the type of courses they want. Students can choose from a list of as many as 100 courses at HBS – with the additional opportunity to cross register for some courses at other faculties at Harvard or MIT (though getting the schedules aligned for this might be complicated).

The process of selecting between the 100 plus courses[103] can be tricky. And competition to enroll in some of the 'star' courses can be fierce. To align capacity with demand, HBS uses the allocation algorithm described previously to assign courses to students. However, things are not as simple as ranking courses from most important to least relevant. There are several other considerations, such as the reputation of different professors teaching the same course and choose specific time slots to avoid overlapping courses. And then there are other scheduling problems – do you choose the class you are really interested in, even though it starts at 8:30 in the morning? Or would you rather try to have every Friday afternoon off? Quite the headache. So how do you make sure you trick the HBS algorithm into giving you exactly what you want?

All this leads to a relatively complex allocation process for courses. I spent a lot of time devising different strategies for course allocation, taking into account different factors, such as preferred courses but also avoiding gaps in between courses of a couple of hours. I lived off campus, so that would have been a very inefficient use of time in an era when there is not a lot to spare.

HBS operates on two schedules: the X and the Y schedule. Courses on the X schedule fall on Mondays, Tuesdays and occasionally on Wednes-

---

103   113 to be exact – find an overview on **http://goo.gl/chn5nG**

days. Y schedule courses fall on Thursdays and Fridays and the alternate Wednesday. Students need to select a minimum number of courses in each schedule. Some courses have prerequisites that need to be fulfilled (i.e. a specific course would need to be completed prior to applying for this course). Then the same course might be taught by different professors, and you may want a particular member of the faculty. Also, some courses are only available in either the fall or winter schedule. Depending on how the algorithm runs, that might dramatically impact your initial strategy! Finally, some courses end the year with an exam – others require students to write a paper. Ideally, you might want to balance those out – you don't want to end up having to write 6 papers a semester. And did I mention you have 'half' classes? You need to fit two of them into your schedule to make up for a full class.

This ended up being so complex that I tried to optimize it by downloading all of the data from the online registration tool in Excel and wrote a VBA code to help me devise my course selection strategy[104]. My automated Excel sheet enabled me to have a preview of my schedule depending on how the simulation would work out. Proud as a peacock, I sent in my allocation based on my own simulation environment, only to find out later that I did not beat the algorithm – my VBA-driven strategies had kind of failed me. Better luck next time!

53

So HBS has award-winning algorithms... what's the deal with all of these lotteries?

Despite having this great algorithm, HBS tends to use two other systems for resource allocation. There is the 'First Come First Serve' system (used for signing up for lunch sessions with professors for instance, or for getting tickets to parties), and then there is the (in)famous lottery system. Despite the algorithm, the latter option still remains popular at HBS and decides on

---

104 VBA – Visual Basic for Applications is a programming language in Microsoft Excel.

slightly less impactful, though important, allocations. An overview of some of the lotteries I participated in:

- Small group breakfast sessions with Dean Nohria (I was IN!)
- The opportunity for a guided tour of the brand new Tata center on the HBS campus (Didn't make it)
- A new class on communication skills, introduced in the middle of the second term of EC year, to be taught by Professor Timothy McCarthy (a visiting star professor of the Harvard Kennedy School whose communications class is massively oversubscribed – I was IN!)
- A behind-the-scenes visit to Logan airport in Boston organized by the Aerospace and Aviation Club at HBS (Didn't make it)
- The classes offered through the Spotlight series (read more in the next chapter) (IN!)
- And much, much more

Although it often worked to my advantage, I am not a big fan of the lottery system. One just doesn't seem to have any form of control, which makes you feel powerless. At the end of the day, HBS could consider admitting students to its MBA program using a lottery system?!? – perhaps, with the low probability of being admitted to HBS, it might come across a bit as a lottery anyway?

54

HBS Spotlight series – what job are students hiring HBS for?

Some of HBS's key assets are their professors. During my first months in school, I had the opportunity to attend a talk from Clay Christensen[105]. He is one of the star professors at HBS and one of the world's top experts on in-

---

105 See him in action on another topic in a TEDx-talk here: **http://goo.gl/W49Ftb**

novation and growth. One of his messages that stuck with me is that when you are selling a product, a service or yourself to customers, other businesses or friends and family, you have to ask yourself the following question: "What is the job this product would be hired to do?" Or, on a personal level, "What is the job my wife/husband hired me to do?" So here's a question: What do students hire HBS for? Is it to get that high paying job? That network that will serve them for the rest of their lives? To have the perfect excuse to spend two jolly years of life? Or do students actually value the quality of the academic content of the HBS MBA program?

In my experience, students in the program are serious about taking advantage of the excellent professors at HBS and their teaching. Take the following example: in mid-May 2013, only a couple of weeks before the end of my first year at HBS, and at a time when all students were selecting their second year courses, a petition was circulated amongst the HBS student body. The petition claimed that HBS students "recognize and are delighted that HBS places a strong commitment to teaching," but also that "many of the hallmark professors who we consider thought leaders in their respective industries ... are not teaching next year. After analyzing the course evaluations, it is our understanding that 34% of the classes that were offered this past academic calendar year, which had an instructor effectiveness rating of 6.5 or above (out of 7.0), will no longer be taught by these professors (or taught at all) next year." Besides the petition, a list of names and profiles of the targeted professors was distributed. The star professors on this list were Clayton Christensen[106] (remember him?), Youngme Moon[107],

---

106 **http://goo.gl/OtbvOm**

107 **http://goo.gl/u7zysv**

Deepak Malhotra[108], Joe Lassiter[109], Jan Rivkin[110] and Yuhai Xuan.[111]

About ten days later, on May 25th, the president of the HBS Student Association sent out an email which seemed like the HBS administration's response to the petition. "We wanted to send out a quick note to clarify some information regarding the EC course selection process … It was stated in the petition that roughly a third of the top rated professors from last year would not be teaching in the EC next year. The admin looked further into that number and, in fact, the correct number is roughly 13% (i.e., roughly 13% of last year's faculty with rankings over 6.5 will not be teaching next year). This sort of turnover is normal and happens every year – the circumstances involving those faculty members range from personal health concerns to increased non-teaching duties. We have also learned that there are several faculty members rotating back into the EC, who are equally regarded as rock star professors when they left the EC years ago and will now be back in the classroom. … All said, we are working with the Student Association Senate and faculty to provide ECs with the opportunity to learn from some of the popular professors who are not teaching a course this year."

And then, there was silence…

Until November 6th, when all students received a new communication from the Student Association, stating that "the Student Association is excited to announce The Spotlight Series, beginning in December. This programming is intended to act as a supplement to the EC curriculum and to provide exposure to professors who are not teaching EC courses this year. We will be offering three different seminars this year, led by Professors Jan

---

108   **http://goo.gl/H0737y**
109   **http://goo.gl/baqrYG**
110   **http://goo.gl/xM51j5**
111   No longer at HBS.

108   109

110

Rivkin, Deepak Malhotra and Clayton Christensen (remember him again?).”

Victory for the student body? Or just a little sweetener offered by the HBS administration? Or a fair compromise? I guess it all depends what one is actually attending HBS for… or what one is hiring HBS for…

My personal view is that the teaching quality of a professor is a very important parameter in the selection of classes. Most of the pure class content can easily be gathered through different sources. The actual learning experience from experts and excellent teachers is unique. Think about it as watching a captive TED talk of an amazing speaker. The content of their speech is probably available in dozens of books and research papers… or online. But the way in which a great speaker presents and delivers that information is what makes it unique and memorable. That's why I signed up for the spotlight series – all of them. And while some students might consider the Spotlight Series additional extracurricular case work, I enjoyed the learning experience very much. Time spent with the Clays, the Deepaks and the Jans of this world is time well spent. And it is time spent on what I personally hired HBS for.

55

HBS conferences

I had a guest staying at my place one weekend – a friend pursuing a PhD in Chicago who flew to Boston to present at a scientific conference. And as I was heading to a conference that weekend myself (the Harvard European conference – I went there as an attendee however, not a speaker), I reflected on the multitude of conferences held at Boston and Harvard every weekend. I counted a total of 24 conferences in an academic year at HBS alone. Topics ranged from the Retail and Luxury Conference to the Design Conference to the Latin America Conference. Competition between conferences is fierce. The weekend my friend came to visit, attendees had to choose between the European and the overlapping Venture Capital & Private Equity conference. Seems to me like Harvard does suffer from 'conferencitis'.

Conferences at HBS are organized by student clubs. Most of the graduate programs at Harvard are spread over two years, assuring a handover of conference knowledge from one year to the other between student members of the clubs. The second year students 'teach' the first year students the nitty-gritty of running the club and organizing conferences. As this system ensures continuity, many conferences within the Harvard community have created a strong legacy and brand name for themselves, attracting hundreds of participants (both students but also many professionals) and generous sponsors year after year. Moreover, the strength of the Harvard brand name is also an asset in mobilizing top speakers from all over the world without providing them with any kind of compensation. For most of the speakers, it's an honor to speak at Harvard. Speakers include (former) presidents, CEOs of S&P 500 companies and inspiring entrepreneurs. No wonder most conferences attract a crowd.

Conferences at HBS are not free, however. Participants have to budget between $15 and $150 for a ticket, depending on the conference AND your link to the school (discounts are available for students). With these price levels and the support of sponsoring deals with the more renowned consultancies of this world, the profitability of the conferences is guaranteed. Moreover, as costs for organizing clubs are often limited to marketing and operational expenses, the income generated through conferences is the lifeline of the HBS student clubs. That money can then be wisely invested in organizing all kinds of other events for the benefit of club members.

Are these conferences all about creating awesome networking opportunities? Or are they Harvard money-making machines for the student clubs? Is their main goal to provide students with resume filling opportunities? Do they aim to provide a strong platform for learning? I'd argue it's a bit of everything. And whatever their main attraction might be, the continued popularity of these conferences both within and outside the Cambridge student community proves their value. And who knows, maybe one day, I will be the one invited to speak at a Harvard conference. It would definitely be an honor.

PART VII

SOME OF THE DEFINING
MOMENTS AT HBS

56

The international student – the documentation issue

A first defining moment at HBS for international students starts before the commencement of school. While trying to be as international as possible, HBS is still on U.S. soil – and the U.S. immigration is probably one of the strictest and most well-organized immigration services in the world. Although being admitted to Harvard definitely helps with the paperwork for the U.S., it still remains quite a hassle to get all the paperwork correct and on time. Even for me, planning to move to the U.S. from a Western European country, it was a pain to sort out – I can only imagine the difficulties people from other continents must have gone through to get the right documents to the right place at the right time.

HBS students from outside the U.S. can apply for an F1 or J1 visa. The most common one is the F1-visa, which is basically a student visa. Students are allowed to live in the U.S. for the length of their studies, but are not allowed to work in the U.S. (some exceptions aside – e.g. on campus work paid for by the school). Partners of HBS students can also receive a visa. The J1 visa is more common for students on specific government-backed programs.

While demanding, the process for getting the visa is well-documented and pretty straightforward. It requires a lot of documents, a couple hundred dollars and a trip to a U.S. embassy for an interview. The embassy will then hold on to your passport for a couple of weeks and send it back to you by mail with a U.S. visa in it.

Upon arrival in the U.S., international students need to go to the Harvard International Office[112] to get their documents validated. Upon receiving this final stamp, I was legally allowed to live in the U.S. for the period of my studies. (Note that you need to get your paperwork revalidated by Harvard on a yearly basis – something I forgot to do – which almost got me into trouble when I returned to the U.S. after a trip home).

---

112   Find out more about the Harvard International Office (HIO) at **http://goo.gl/noqvaA**

At the end of the day, I had two types of official documents granted to me by the embassy – one is the visa I mentioned above that is directly incorporated into the passport. The other one is a set of three papers (A4-sized) stapled together with a set of codes and signatures on them. Oddly, in my two years living in and traveling to the U.S., the visa in my passport didn't seem to affect my entry to the country. On the other hand, the (very unhandy) set of A4-sized papers (also known as the I-20 form) were key for getting access to the U.S. After some traveling, these papers were literally starting to fall apart. This got me into trouble at one point, and I was taken to the back offices of Border Security at Boston airport. After that experience, I immediately got new papers issued.

Once on American soil, I quickly came to realize that as an average student in the U.S. (who likes to have a drink once in a while), paperwork remains important. As the legal age to drink is 21, bars, restaurants and liquor stores don't take any risk of losing their liquor license and hence check anyone who looks under 35 years old! With the face of a young man, I got 'carded' all the time, meaning I had to show them my passport so they could validate my age. This meant having to take my passport with me all the time when going for dinner/drinks. Luckily, the state of Massachusetts (home to Boston) issues what they call liquor IDs. These are the size of a credit card, and are accepted everywhere as proof that you are of drinking age. I later found out they can even be used as a means of identification for domestic flights!

57

TOM – jumping cranberries! And Other Star Cases...

HBS students enrolled in the full-time MBA program are going to read hundreds of cases during their two year tenure at the school. And while most of the specifics of these cases are long forgotten even before leaving the environment of the school, some will stay with us for the rest of our lives.

As it turns out, there are not only star professors at HBS – there are also star cases. Find an overview below:

The jumping cranberries of TOM[113] – In our operations class, there is this one business case on jumping cranberries. The featured company lets the cranberries fall from a certain height to see if they 'jump'. Bouncing cranberries are deemed to be of good quality. The ones that do not bounce are filtered out of the production process[114]. It is a case in which students are introduced to several aspects of operations management such as capacity and bottleneck management. This case is a real HBS classic (just try imagining thousands of jumping cranberries). It is humorously referred to throughout life at HBS and is duly joked about in Skydeck sessions and HBS Shows. But most of all, it was one of the hardest cases in our TOM course to crack, and left many students without any prior supply chain experience with difficult formulas and bad headaches…

Heidi Roizen of LEAD[115] – During our leadership class, we discussed the case of Heidi Roizen. She is a strong businesswoman who made her mark in corporate life. Students discuss the case, but are then confronted with an interesting reality at the end of class[116]. Heidi remains the talk of the town in a lot of later classes.

The Boston Chickens of FRC[117] – In our accounting class, we had a case on Boston Chicken. It is probably one of my favorite HBS cases and was very informative on how a seemingly successful and fast-growing company was using interesting accounting techniques to make things look great indeed! A real eye-opener!

Getting drunk during FRC – Another accounting class. The whisky-making company Compass Box is a case all students remember for the simple reason that it is all about whisky!

Watching a movie during LEAD – 12 angry men – This leadership class, spread over two sessions, is all about watching and discussing what happens in the movie 12 Angry Men, a classic from the fifties starring Henry Fonda. And who doesn't enjoy watching a movie during class for a change?

---

113 TOM is short for Technology and Operations Management – Find out more on all courses in HBS's required curriculum here: **http://goo.gl/TnGb7E**
114 Shapiro, Roy D. "National Cranberry Cooperative, 1996." Harvard Business School Case 688-122, May 1988. (Revised July 2011.)
115 LEAD is short for Leadership and Organizational Behaviour.
116 I won't tell what exactly – don't want to spoil it for fresh HBS admits!
117 FRC is short for Financial Reporting and Control.

Erik Peterson in LEAD – Another leadership class classic about a young professional gone all wrong. Isn't there a little Erik Peterson in all of us?

Alcohol again, but now in MKT[118] – Reviewing the marketing strategy of a fine wine-maker Chateau Margaux! Yet another HBS classic on alcohol!

Fast food in our Finance II class – Burger King – also a personal favorite. What should have been a 'feel good' story about Burger King (since a lot of people made a lot of money) was kind of a 'feel bad' story for me (as I didn't see it coming even after reading the case). Am I any good at evaluating the value of businesses? Quite the wake-up call for me.

Rent-The-Runway in TEM[119] – We discussed the young company Rent-The-Runway (RTR) in our entrepreneurship class. RTR is a real HBS breed – it is a young fashion company founded by two former HBS students during their time at HBS. They are now case protagonists in their very own HBS case and it was a pleasure having them in class discussing their experiences.

58

ALD – don't cry for me HBS

An ALD class (short for Authentic Leadership Development) is not the typical HBS class. Indeed, if there is one thing students tend to associate the ALD classes with, it is… crying. A lot of tears are shed during parts of this class. It is a remarkable experience to see HBS students, who are often expected to be strong and fearless leaders, talk about their doubts and fears, and do so in the most emotional kind of way.

The ALD class has become a HBS classic. HBS has always been on the forefront of topics related to leadership (though this one is about being an authentic leader, not just a leader). However, it could be considered a bit surprising that touchy-feely ALD has become a top elective for students.

HBS offers nine (!) ALD classes taught by four different professors, and most of them fill up rather quickly. It is a class purely focused on soft-skills

---

118 MKT is short for Marketing.
119 TEM is short for The Entrepreneurial Manager – it is a course on entrepreneurship.

and identifying one's inner self, personal challenges and motivations in life. It is based on the principle that in order to have impact on the world surrounding us, we first need to understand and acknowledge who we are and what we want and need from life.

In this class, students are told to open their hearts and share some of their deepest thoughts, aspirations and fears with other students. Every afternoon following the group class session, students gather in assigned groups of six and receive an assignment to discuss personal topics within the safe environment of that group. Students then have to reflect on how they felt during that session by uploading a report on a secure website to which only the class professor has access[120].

I was surprised by how much people were willing to share in these small groups of six (complete strangers prior to the first meeting). The assignments can be very personal in nature and, if done properly, push students toward sharing some of their most personal thoughts and feelings. Students discuss how they lost a loved one, tell about their difficult youth or just share the joy of being in a new relationship. Topics are broad and diverse – but they all have one thing in common: they are authentic. And yes, this invariably leads to tears once in a while. At the same time, it is amazing how powerful it is to have 'strangers' listen to your life stories, provide you with new ways of thinking and offer genuine, unbiased feedback.

Besides the small group discussions, there are also the academic full group class sessions. While I found the small group discussions to be extremely powerful, I found the full group sessions to be a total waste of time. Those sessions were full of clichés. And most of the time, we were kicking in open doors[121].

As a guide, we were using Bill George's book True North[122]. The book contains the personal stories of tons of leaders and CEOs and explains how

---

120 A lot of emphasis was put on the safety of the upload tool, as it was rumored that in previous years, an issue with the security settings allowed other students were able to read the reports of their fellow students by mistake!

121 I know this doesn't make any sense in English – I translated an expression literally from my mother tongue (Dutch). It basically means stating the obvious! An example would be to say that to win a soccer game, you need to make more goals than the other team.

122 Bill George, Peter Sims, and David Gergen, True North: Discover Your Authentic Leadership, New York: Jossey-Bass, 2007

'being authentic' made them so successful. I was not a fan of the book. I believe one doesn't necessarily need a book full of CEO stories to identify authentic behavior. Also, I interacted with one of the CEOs described in the book, and the experience left me feeling very confused. The person I had talked to was a totally different person from the one described in the book. I felt the stories in the book seemed more like a marketing campaign for their persona than an authentic reflection of their personalities. But then again, who am I to critique top-notch CEOs…

Overall, ALD was one of my favorite classes, despite hating the book and the full group sessions. I loved the small group sessions and will never forget some of the stories I heard and some of the emotions I witnessed. I too had some very emotional moments during those sessions and shared more than I thought possible. On top of that, I was pushed outside of my comfort zone beyond the group sessions, as some of the exercises we had to do involved talking to random strangers in the street about their life stories and telling the people close to you why you love them so much. Whether we like it or not, I believe the single most interesting thing in life are other human beings and the set of emotions that surround them; hence my love for ALD and having it as part of the defining moments at HBS.

59

Schultz is a hypocrite (and other comments in class that were worth writing down)

I got into the habit of writing down some of the interesting and/or unusual things that were said in class, either by students or professors, and occasionally by class guests. I also recorded some quotes from professors that I found interesting on the last few pages of my class notebooks.

Most of these comments were made in a funny/humorous setting, and taking them out of context might make some of them sound weird or even offensive – however, they may be worth reviewing, as they can give a sense of what's going on at HBS and the kinds of discussions taking place. Unfortunately, I didn't always take note of who the comment came from – apologies for the missing info. Find an overview of the last few pages of my HBS notebooks below.

"Hitler was a lot like Clinton." (we were talking soft skills for the record)

"Don't believe in happiness, it is a by-product of satisfaction."

"Better to have them inside the tent peeing out, than outside the tent peeing in." (on the importance of having people around the table when negotiating – key learning of my negotiations class)

"Feel the fear and do it anyway." (Stuart Thorn, CEO Southwire)

"You can't be a champion if you personalize everything that is going wrong." (something I tend to do – so was a strong message for me)

"We are trained to think in two dimensions and two axes, though most systems do not fall back on initial state."

"The budgeting process should focus on what is right, not who is right."

"Leaders are made – not born." (Professor Nancy Koehn – teaching the power and glory class at HBS)

"It is better to be kind than to be right."

"Choose your primary customer – treat all the other ones just good enough." (Professor Robert Simmons)

"Hope is the belief in the plausibility of the possible as opposed to the necessity of the possible." (Maimonides)

"Give a man a fish – he will have food for a day. Teach a man how to fish – you just lost your leverage." (quote made by a finance professor – don't make yourself dispensable!)

"The only question you need to ask yourself – how does a company compete?"

"To be successful in life, all you need is a great theory and a tiny little bit of proof that it actually works in real life."

"I can resist anything but temptations." – Oscar Wilde (how will we ever solve unethical behavior?!?)

"You condemn those selling guns, but you are killing people yourself by selling fat making products." (HBS student to Howard Schultz, CEO of Starbucks. Quite the comment to make to such a successful CEO!)

"In preparation for battle, plans are useless but planning is indispensable." – Dwight D Eisenhower.

"The mouse has no agent." – Warren Buffet (on why he'd invested so much in Disney)

"Suffering from brain drain is better than putting the brain in the drain." (on discussing why developing countries should continue to invest massively in education, despite seeing a lot of their educated work force leave the country)

"The rich try to avoid boredom." (Henrik Ibsen – when discussing a case on Norway and why they do what they do)

"There are only two mistakes you can make in a supply chain: making too much or making too little." (Who said supply chain management was complex?!?)

"There are no rules at Harvard, but a lot of norms." (huh!?!)

60

My big fat simulation

Most of the students' time is spent solving business cases in the Aldrich classrooms, but students are also exposed to interesting simulations designed by the HBS administration. Some are part of the larger FIELD program; others are extensions to existing courses. The most memorable of all simulations is definitely the TOM Shad simulation. TOM is short for Technology and Operations Management – it is the operations class at HBS. Shad is the name of the gym building that is redressed into a huge simulated production hall for two days a year. It is the first simulation of the HBS MBA program and occurs very soon after the start of the program.

The TOM Shad simulation is one that forces a lot of HBS students to do something they might never have done before – manual labor! Indeed, the simulation requires students to create their own little production chain of circuit boards. Students have to organize and run a production line after which they will be judged based on the number of items produced, number of quality defects and amount of inventory used/produced. After the first run (during which a lot of things tend to go wrong), students get the chance to change their production processes in order to optimize the results. Not surprisingly, by applying some of the techniques taught during the course, most teams manage to dramatically improve their performance compared to the first run.

The interesting part of the TOM Shad simulation is not the simulation itself, but all the preparatory work that goes into it. It is the first time students work closely together in small groups with other section mates. We had to choose a leader, we had to agree on how we would operate our production line, we had to decide who would make the required calculations for the exercise and send in reports to the professors. It was a good introduction to group work at HBS: strong personalities all put together in a team, having to work towards a common goal. Happy to say that my group did very well on this exercise!

Another simulation that was eye-opening to me was the LEAD[123] Everest Simulation. In teams of six, students have to simulate the climb to the top of Mount Everest through a computer platform, with each student being assigned a specific profile and a specific challenge. I don't want to give away any of the goals or insights I got from this exercise, but it was a great experience. In a 3-hour session, I discovered more flaws in my way of working and communication than I had in a full year before this simulation[124].

There was another interesting simulation as part of our strategy class. In small groups, we had to decide how we wanted to run a hardware company – how much would we produce? At what price? Do we want to introduce new products or milk older models of your product? Not only was it fun – I seemed pretty good at it! My group won that simulation by the way! The one question remains – how well of a substitute are simulations for real life? I believe simulations are only as valuable as the insights they give. For that reason, the LEAD simulation had the most important impact on me, as it challenged my soft kills more than my hard skills. Or maybe I just preferred a career as climber of the Everest to a "Green Wire Officer" during the TOM Shad Simulation...

---

123 LEAD is short for Leadership and Organizational Behavior.
124 I 'died' on my way to the top of Everest because of this...

61

FIELD2 in Ghana: in the name of the rose!

I spent 10 days in Ghana, Africa as part of the FIELD2 course at HBS – a course aimed at immersing first year MBA students in business within a developing country. Students are randomly grouped in teams of six and are assigned to a global partner – a senior executive of a local business. The aim of FIELD2 is to help the global business partners develop a new product or service customized to their local market. As such, we dedicated most of our time in Ghana on market research.

I loved the project I was working on. Our global partner was a Ghanaian toilet paper manufacturer that used to be the only toilet paper company in the market until Ghana was flooded by Chinese imports ten to fifteen years ago. The company had to find new ways of dealing with this competition. The goal of our project was to develop innovative ideas to help them avoid getting into financial 'shit' – get it!?!

Due to the nature of the product, the team I was working with quickly became very close. There might not be a better team building exercise than to discuss one's toilet experiences in detail with others... or to spend hours in markets and slums in and around Accra (Ghana's capital city) surveying people on what made them choose one or the other type of toilet paper.

Visiting the factory was enjoyable. Having worked in a manufacturing environment before (in Europe), I loved seeing how the factory was organized and operated. I was amazed by how efficient it was despite the weary state of some of the machines. When I asked how old the paper-making machine was, they told me it was installed in the seventies. 'Oh, so it's like more than 40 years old," I said. "No no," the manager replied, "It has been here for 40 years. We bought it second hand from a company in the UK back then. Nobody really knows how old it actually is."

I was also astonished by the amount of scrap the factory produced, i.e. products that had to be discarded because of quality or other issues. On top of that, they struggled to find reliable suppliers. Their oil supplier occasionally supplied product of inferior quality (hence affecting production and product quality). Their suppliers of recycled paper often left them paperless (because they could make more money selling it in the harbor to ships heading off to China where they could use the paper as well) or ripped them off by mixing plastic and other junk in the paper supply. And the employees held a lot of power in the factory – I was told the story of the previous plant director LITERALLY being thrown out of the factory by disgruntled employees. Now that's a tough place to do business! I had a lot of respect for the people running the place and trying to make the best of it every day. And did I mention the continuous power cuts disrupting production?

Besides production issues, the market place was not very friendly either. Markets in Accra are flooded with cheap Chinese imports. However, our market research revealed why the local brand was able to survive for so long. First, it dissolved easily in the toilet, which is really important in a country with poor sewage infrastructure. Second, it was more absorbent than other brands. Finally, it was packaged individually, as such easily catering to a population that often only had the finances to buy one roll at a time.

I also loved the interactions with local Ghanaians. I remember our very first visit to the toilet paper company, when one of the factory workers took the hand of the manager we were talking to. I figured they were man and wife. Turns out, they are just colleagues, and holding hands is a normal way of showing affection between friends in parts of Africa. I was impressed by the resilience of the Ghanaians. In less than 10 days, I had two taxis and a bus break down. However, everything got fixed and worked out fine… albeit with some delays…. Delays actually don't even matter, as planning transportation in Accra is a lost cause. Traffic is horrific and unpredictable. The same trip might take 20 minutes one day and more than two hours the next day. Hence breakdowns are just part of the variability in transportation times. In the end, we always reached our final destination.

I loved how nice the average Ghanaian was. While most of them live off $50 a month or less, they are very kind and optimistic people. They were so agreeable that it even interfered with our market research when doing our survey on the 'Rose' toilet paper brand. Instead of giving the constructive feedback or criticism we were looking for, they would just tell us that they would switch to 'Rose' next time around… just to be nice… but NOT exactly the answers we were looking for to progress with our market research…

Finally, I loved the group I was working with. They were a fun bunch of people and while great to work with, they were even better to hang out with. I adored my whole Ghana experience – it was unique and enriching in so many ways. Thank you HBS. Thank you Ghana! Go Rose!

62

Ain't no party like a Euro Club party

Some would say HBS is really all about the parties and the relationships created with others at those parties. HBS party life starts even before the official HBS start and continues long after graduation. A couple of days before my start at HBS, the HBS Student Association (SA) launched the first official party called the 'White Party'. As its name states, the SA invited all fresh new HBS students (and their partners or families) to the Spangler lawn on campus for drinks, snacks and music – as long as you were dressed in white!

The SA repeats a similar initiative early in the year by throwing a large (free) party for all new HBS students. The party took place in the Boston Courthouse, a very nice location for what would be a HBS freshmen casino evening full of animation, music and drinks. While no real money was at stake, students with the highest amount of chips at the end of the night could win some prizes offered by the SA. But what really mattered was to mingle with the other classmates and get to know as many people as possible. It was a fun who-is-who kind of evening, where I was still struggling with names / faces / accents.

Once the academic year gets going, it is the clubs that take over most of the party-organizing work. HBS parties tend to be the most important source of income for most clubs, and some have a more vested interest in them than others. The one club that has a strong reputation to host some of the most infamous parties at HBS, is the Euro Club, starting with the Beach Party at the beginning of the year.

Some parties also are the object of a lot of controversy. Every year, the HBS Australia and New Zealand Club organizes the Priscilla Ball, a theme party inspired by the movie the Adventures of Priscilla, Queen of the Desert, featuring drag queens and transgender women. Students will meticulously prepare for this party, with all men dressing up like women (think dresses and nylon stockings) and women suiting up like men. It is, to my knowledge, the only party at HBS where taking pictures or videos for that matter, is strictly forbidden – God forbid that some of the future CEOs or members of congress would have to explain some of these pictures to the press one day. But it seems that the days of this HBS tradition are numbered, as the ball has been subject to more and more criticism even from within the HBS community – does the Priscilla Ball still have its place in the inclusive environment that HBS wants to be?[125]

Some other blockbuster parties are the Newport Ball (held in a castle in nearby Newport), Holidazzle (generally hosted at a hotel in Boston) and of course the HBS graduation party. My class of 2014 had its graduation party in the Prudential Tower (Pru) – one of the iconic buildings of Boston. The party was hosted at the Top of the Hub, on one of the top floors of the Pru with an amazing view over the city. Students were nicely dressed, there was music, food and dancing. And also a lot of goodbyes to people that I knew I would probably never see or meet again. More than graduation day itself, this party felt like the end of my MBA experience. It was the last time I put my tux on for a party, last time I danced with some of my fellow students and the last time I kind of sneaked out to go home at one point, not being very fond of goodbyes. Bye bye HBS.

---

125 Note that my MBA class of 2014 had the first transgender woman ever at HBS amongst it ranks.

63

FIELD3 – the cradle for the next Facebook!?!

What would you do if someone handed you $5,000 to start a business – no questions asked? Seems great, no? Well, that's exactly what the FIELD3 program is all about. As part of the curriculum, HBS students have to start a company in groups of six. And this time, students can choose freely who they want to team up with, unlike for other exercises or for FIELD2. HBS provides the check of $5,000 per team and off you go! Each team gets 10 days to come up with a broad business idea which they then have to present to students of another section. It will be the start of a couple of intense weeks with money in the bank... for now...

Besides having to worry about your company and its future, HBS found an interesting way to spice things up. Your $5,000 is not completely free – you will have to report back to your investors! And your investors are... the students of another section! All students have to present their ideas/companies to that other section. Those students will then trade the stocks of your company on an online trading platform. The system is pretty advanced and allows for buying and shorting[126] stocks.

I in turn had another section present their business ideas to me. This time, I was on the investors' side. After the presentations ended, the investing madness started on the online trading platform. All the teams that presented got assigned a ticker symbol reflected in the online simulation tool. Each stock had a starting value of $100. For the next 3 hours, students would have the chance to buy and sell stocks, depending on how much they believed in the potential success of those companies (or how much they thought other students believed in the potential success of the business). Once the trading started, students could see the price of stock go up and down in real time (based on market demand and supply). Students are incentivized to invest in the 'right' stock, as a team of HBS professionals

---

126   Shorting stocks is the process of selling stocks you don't own, in the hope that prices will go down so you can buy the stocks again later at a discount to make a profit.

will rate the business ideas and their execution within a couple of months. The teams with the best ideas, according to the HBS jury, will receive a good grade. Those students that invested heavily into stocks with a good review would receive good grades as well.

I remember how stressed I felt during the trading exercise. I didn't really care about my grade so much, but I loved the whole exercise of taking bets on a company which would outperform the others on our local HBS stock market. I shorted the ones I believed were crap, invested massively in the ones I believed had potential. And I had great fun. Never before had I been active as a trader, or a venture capitalist for that matter! I remember meeting up with my girlfriend for dinner after the first hour of trading (after which most trading activity had ended) and how I just kept on trading on the online platform using my phone. I was addicted! The fact that I had been making a lot of money with my initial trades had probably fed that addiction – it was like being on the winning hand in a casino!

At the end of the day, the market closed for 2 months. During that time, the teams would have the chance to work on their ideas. They would then present progress and financials again to the section investors, after which there would be another trading simulation (starting where the last trading results left off). And then there was D-day. The teams that had proven to be great at executing their ideas (as reflected in their final market value in the trading tool) would have the chance to present to a selected jury of HBS alums. That jury would determine which company would receive the highest honor of winning the FIELD3 competition. They would judge the companies on finances, execution, the idea itself, and of course on the potential and scalability of it.

In a big final event, in front of a full auditorium, the final winner was announced: EasyBioData, a match-making service for the Indian matrimonial search market. Find out more about them online. FIELD3 has some interesting financials to it. First, HBS spent about $750,000 on this program – or $5,000 for 150 teams[127]. The financial return of that investment (as measured by the cumulated revenues of all the companies

---

127 This is an estimate I made. Some teams did not spend their full $5,000, other teams got additional cash based on reviews during the project.

started compared to the investment done) was negative – it was a hugely loss-making venture. Second, it is interesting to see how different teams spent their money. Some invested in assets that they were trying to rent out to make money. One team had a very different approach, in spending nearly their full budget on a marketing company to bring traffic to their website (their online traffic stats were amazing). And then there were those that were more frugal with their budgets – barely spending half of what they had been allocated.

There were some successes coming from the FIELD exercise that were intangible – there were the invaluable lessons learned by students AND the fact that some of the FIELD3 companies are now successful start-ups. Check out HourlyNerd for instance![128] Congrats guys!

Is FIELD3 really worth the investment for HBS? Do other channels, such as the new venture competition, not suffice? In that competition, students can freely choose to start a company and apply for financial aid, professional coaching and legal support. Is that not a better and wiser way to spend that amount of money? Well, while FIELD3 cost me a lot of time, energy and headaches, I do believe the lessons learned were very valuable. It made me realize how difficult it is to make a living outside of a regular job or corporate life. I also understood the limitations of entrepreneurship and why entrepreneurship would be a good or bad idea for me. And finally, I discovered I could get addicted to playing on the stock market – so I'd better stay away from it… I believe FIELD3, with some minor adjustments, should remain part of the HBS curriculum. And I'm sure HBS can spare the yearly $750,000 to do so. And if anything, it supports the local Cambridge economy, as tons of services were launched for website and app development for FIELD3. Maybe those guys are the real entrepreneurs…

---

128 HourlyNerd raised a lot of money and has become an interesting player in the freelance and consultancy marketplace.

64

And my winner is... BGIE!?

As my first year at the Harvard Business School (HBS) was coming to an end, I started reflecting on which classes had been most valuable to me. In RC year, there are five classes per semester and therefore a total of 10 a year. Looking back, I found all of the classes interesting in one way or the other, but some definitely stood out. Moreover, the rating of classes is heavily impacted by the quality of the individual professors. Three classes stood out to me – my personal winners being BGIE, STRAT and FRC[129].

How about starting a class with the professor asking: "What are the goals of the European Union? What do they want to achieve?" Or consider questions such as "Can one rationalize a government saving surplus in a foreign currency compared to investing it in the future human/financial capital of the country?" If you know all the answers to that, the BGIE course (short for Business, Government and International Economy) might not be interesting to you at all. If not, and if you have any interest in how political and macro-economic factors impact conducting business in different parts of the world, then BGIE might be one of your favorite classes as well.

A typical BGIE case covers the European debt crisis, the fast-growing economy of Brazil or the unique economics of oil-exporting countries such as Nigeria and Saudi Arabia. However, less publicized and therefore less well-known topics are also addressed, such as the political situation in Uganda and the management of copper resources in Chile. This latter case being one of my all-time favorite cases, as it tried to address the question I asked earlier on how to manage the budget surplus in a time when copper prices are high.

I loved this course for several reasons. First of all, it really helped me to gain a better understanding of some of the political/economic tension

---

129   BGIE, STRAT and FRC are courses of the required curriculum at HBS and respectively stand for Business, Government and the International Economy, Strategy, and Financial Reporting and Control.

that exists on an intra-country level. I feel I now have a grip on the impact of a trade surplus on a country's financials. I loved the professor and the dynamism he brought to the discussions. While BGIE is not a typical business class, it challenged me to think about topics I never thought about before. Quite a challenge – and I love challenges! HBS also underpins the importance of this course for its students, by having it as part of the required curriculum. Second and right after BGIE, is my Strategy class. Led by the globally renowned Professor Jan Rivkin, this class taught me to look at the challenges companies face to ensure their continued existence in the future. It demonstrated the value in understanding and executing one's strategy through some phenomenal cases – my favorite one being the Airbourne Express case, a former package delivery service. I loved how we used simple but effective frameworks to dissect a company in a way that allowed us to propose the best way forward for the company.

Finally, there's FRC, short for Financial Reporting and Control – a fancy name for what is supposed to be an accounting course. How can an accounting class make my top three, you say? Well, the class doesn't focus that much on the more boring parts of accounting. Instead, the course aimed at teaching us how different accounting techniques can be used both in a positive way and in a negative way, i.e. used for the wrong purpose. Yes, we obviously discussed cases on Enron and other accounting fraud. But I mostly enjoyed cases which were in a grey area with regards to the application of accounting standards. In one such case, rather than intentional wrongdoing, the company owners interpreted accounting rules in a different way. Up to us to judge if what they did was really wrong!?!

And then there's the rest of the pack. There's FIN1 and FIN2, focusing on… finance! There's our operations course TOM and our marketing course MKT. We had cases on leadership and ethics under the umbrella of LCA and LEAD. And finally there was TEM, short for The Entrepreneurial Manager, looking at entrepreneurial ventures and the challenges encountered when pursuing that path.[130]

My love for BGIE led me to choose a lot of BGIE-like classes for my EC year. I strongly recommend 'Entrepreneurship and Global Capitalism' and

---

130 For a full overview of the HBS RC courses, look here: **http://goo.gl/TnGb7E**

'The Role of Government in Market Economies' as EC courses. The former helped me understand the evolution of entrepreneurship and globalization over the last 200 years (did you know that our current globalization era is the second one already?), the latter helped me understand key issues related to taxation and subsidy systems and the importance of governments creating the right incentives. Enjoy!

65

W50 – celebrating 50 years of women at HBS

The history and the influence of HBS makes the school a recurrent subject in the press, and from time to time articles can cause some controversy with the general public and HBS students alike. A set of articles in the New York Times (NYT) focused on the gender and class divide at HBS and was a hot topic of discussion on campus[131].

I don't dispute the gender gap issue discussed in the article, and believe that references made in the NYT article are correct (though maybe a bit exaggerated or pulled out of context). However, as a HBS student, I wonder if these gender issues are specific to HBS and if HBS is a specifically hard place for women to thrive compared to other schools or organizations.

Let's look at some numbers. When comparing the percentage of female students admitted to a selection of top business schools in the world, HBS ranks second (only preceded by Wharton). HBS's class of 2015 consists of 40% female students, up from 25% in 1985 and 35% in 2005. The data seems to suggest that while HBS might not have considered the low female to male ratio a priority for decades, they outperform most top business schools today.

I also looked into data related to gender issues on a national level. As HBS is a U.S.-based school with more than 60% American students, I

---

131 Find links to the NYT articles here: **http://goo.gl/VIqrik** and **http://goo.gl/1eq8iG**

131a   131b

expected domestic gender issues to be highly correlated to those at the school. As stated in the World Bank's 2012 global gender report, the U.S. has the 7th highest GDP per capita, but only ranks 22nd on the global gender gap score index[132]. It seems that the gender issues described in the article are more a reflection of U.S. society than HBS specifically. Of course, that doesn't take away HBS's responsibility as a key influencer for (future) society. From what I have seen at HBS, a lot has been done to address gender issues in recent years. As HBS celebrated its 50th anniversary since the first women admitted to HBS, a lot of initiatives had been taken around the gender gap. All students received a HBS W50 T-shirt. The campus was plastered with posters commemorating the anniversary. Finally, and most importantly, a lot of activities and discussion sessions were organized around the W50 theme. I did get frustrated about the latter, as a lot of these discussions turned out to be very sterile. They were often poorly facilitated and dominated by a few people. To avoid any controversy, there was no room in class for remarks outside the set framework or that would not reinforce women's difficulties in society. The discussions were also very U.S.-centric, leaving little to no room for international students from very different backgrounds, cultures and behaviors towards women to share their views and experiences. I would have loved to share some of my experiences from my country (ranked 12th in the gender gap score index – way ahead of the U.S.), but felt uncomfortable doing so.

Some of the smartest people I met at HBS are women. HBS has a key responsibility in creating an environment at the school where gender equality is a priority. The bigger challenge however is to create a society in which that is possible. And that's where all of us share a tremendous responsibility... [133]

---

132 Find full report and definitions used here: **http://goo.gl/L4df6m**
133 Find some interesting articles on how HBS is coping with that challenge here: **http://goo.gl/qPjYLz** and a great article on the first 8 women at HBS here: **http://goo.gl/Fy3zCa**

132

133a

133b

PART

VIII

THE MBA – PAST,
PRESENT, FUTURE

66

The offline MBA – from the classroom
to the real world and back

As I am sipping a coffee at a major coffee chain, I realize that an internal meeting of that coffee shop is going on next to me. As a business school student, I was too curious not to eavesdrop on the conversation. Four staff appeared to be receiving training. I was impressed by the format and professionalism of the meeting. The person I identified as the instructor was sharing ~~Starb~~... the coffee shop's values and priorities, and its key focus on customer happiness. As they discussed these topics, they got occasionally interrupted by another employee, bringing them a variety of cakes and snacks. As the trainees tried the snacks sitting in front of them, they discussed their taste, the content of the cake, and its texture. They even discussed what drink some of these snacks would pair best with. And the discussion was quite lively, I have to say. I was amused when the instructor asked each of them what an ideal snack would look/taste like to them. Now everybody got really excited and launched ideas back and forth. The employees seem really involved.

Interestingly, I was able to link this real life situation to a HBS case study on that company, discussed in class just a couple of days earlier. A big part of the topics that were covered during the typical 80-minute class time were now revealing themselves in front of me. Though this experience may seem trivial, to me it felt as if the paper of my case study had come to life. I was impressed to see how the culture of this organization was actually implemented in real life. And to the credit of the HBS case writers, what I saw correlated very well with the information in the case.

This experience has me thinking about the value of a business education compared to actual real life business experience. One of the premises of an MBA program like HBS's is that the best way to learn about business is to reflect on real life situations from the past, summarized in case studies. Students reflect on the cases, and then discuss their opinions in class among students from very different professional backgrounds and (corporate and social) cultures. This has been key to HBS's teaching method for decades. And HBS seems to have been very successful in selling and delivering this value to their students.

HBS has learned from the success of educating with real business cases. Over the years, they have extended that real life learning beyond their traditional case-based learning method. Proof of that can be found in today's HBS curriculum. There are programs such as IXP, where second year students can participate on projects in different countries around the world. There is the IP (independent project) option, where students work on projects for companies while at HBS, under supervision of HBS professors (receiving credit for the work done). And HBS puts a lot of effort into students finding valuable internships during the first and the second year there. The school also pushes students to engage in clubs and external activities so as to be in touch with the 'outside' business environment. And did I mention the Harvard i-Lab, aiming to support students with entrepreneurial ideas? The most impactful of the changes HBS has implemented in the past couple of years however seems to be the FIELD program (read more about FIELD in other parts of this book). As part of this program, students are required to work on consulting assignments in developing countries around the world, as well as to start their own companies in groups of six. Both the cases and these programs provide a very hands-on exposure to the real life world of business.

This focus on real life problem sets is where the value of an MBA lies for me. I am convinced that the classic business education has to evolve towards more pragmatic and real life learning. I believe this will be to the benefit of the students... and will be a critical parameter for survival of many of the business schools. First, it will become a key differentiator among business schools – most business school programs are very similar, covering more or less the same content ranging from finance to marketing. Second, it is a selling point that the expensive 'offline' MBA programs have against the increasing offer of cheaper online educational offerings. Why spend two years in school (and let go of two years of salary) when most of the content will become available online (and accessible when and where convenient for you)? Third, the changing business environment requires a much more agile and responsive work force. Schools need to prepare their students with more than just fancy finance formulas.

As the meeting of the coffee shop's employees came to an end, I reflected on my learning experience at HBS. HBS is taking the real life learning approach and is expanding upon it with things like the FIELD program. It seems however that some people want to take real life learning even one step further, by stimulating learning solely through practical experiences. At least, that is what Peter Thiel wants to demonstrate through his fellowship[134]. Interesting experiment – future will tell what system is to prevail.

67

HBS HBX

While real life learning plays a prominent role on the HBS campus, don't think that HBS is going to miss out on the online learning boom! It is a business savvy place after all! HBX is HBS's answer to the online education movement. According to the HBX website, it is "a digital learning initiative powered by the faculty of Harvard Business School." HBX is accessible here: **http://goo.gl/jLNktV**.

The main premise of HBX is scale. If a professor at HBS today can have an impact on say 90 students in Boston each time they give a class, a digital version of that same class could reach thousands worldwide at a much lower cost. With the Harvard brand renowned worldwide, the demand for this product could become huge.

As stated by Dean Nohria in an email to the HBS community on the launch of HBX, the following principles were taken into account with the development of HBX:

---

134 The mission of the fellowship of Peter Thiel, co-founder of Paypal, reads as follows: "The Thiel Fellowship gives $100,000 to young people who want to build new things instead of sitting in a classroom." Is this the ultimate form of 'offline' business education?!? Find out more here: **http://goo.gl/W4NtJn**

- HBX must expand the reach of Harvard Business School (as mentioned above)
- HBX must provide faculty with a powerful platform for disseminating their ideas globally
- HBX must complement and enhance our on-campus offerings
- HBX must elevate our reputation for excellence and impact
- HBX offerings must be highly differentiated from existing alternatives
- HBX must be built on a robust and forward-looking economic model

However, HBX might not be as revolutionary as HBS might want to make it sound. EdX, founded by MIT and Harvard in 2013, is an online platform that offers courses ranging from Biology to History. An additional 60 schools have come onboard in just a couple of years. And the courses offered here are FREE! (they try to make money by selling course attendance certificates and other add-on services). And from what I experienced on EdX – it is amazing!

I looked for the infamous CS50 course from Harvard – an introductory course to computer science. The course has become a Harvard classic, and is totally oversubscribed year after year after year. Yet, the EdX platform allows you to follow this course online from your couch, your bed or even your bath (not recommended for safety reasons though) at your pace, in High Definition and for free!

However, HBS decided not to leverage this existing platform and to invest in its own online platform. And there's a couple of important differences between the offers on edX and HBX, the most important one being that HBX is not free – rather it's a platform that provides access to excellent but expensive courses.

The CORe program is the first online offering of HBS on the HBX platform. CORe – short for Credential of Readiness – is HBS's summary on business fundamentals. The tuition fee for the program is $1,800 at the time of writing and people have to apply to be accepted to the program. Students are then assigned to cohorts (HBS's online equivalent of sections) that will go through the program at somewhat the same pace. Unlike EdX, where students are free to look at whatever courses they want, HBX offers a learning platform that is still carefully managed and controlled by HBS. It is an extension of what HBS is doing at its offline campus – not a 'copy-paste' online. To HBS, the focus of HBX seems to be the development of an additional revenue stream. Contrary to EdX, HBX is a purely commercial platform. Which of these models will prevail? Only time will tell. Meanwhile, these evolutions leave us with some online food for thought…

68

The online MBA – professors at HBS disagree (Porter vs Christensen)

One of the key theories taught at HBS is called "disruptive innovation." This theory, developed and published by star-professor Clay Christensen, aims to explain how certain industries and blue chip companies found themselves almost eradicated in no time, while others managed to maintain their power position by being aware of the danger of disruption and acting upon it. Another star professor at HBS is Michael Porter, considered a key authority with everything that has to do with corporate strategy and competitiveness.

So here we are today, with HBS having to respond to key challenges in its business model that is about to be disrupted by the Internet – or not? Will the future of the MBA (or of education for that matter) be online? Other schools and other Harvard faculties have moved aggressively towards the web. HBS, having a very different model of education based on classroom discussion around cases, was until recently holding its guns. That was until Dean Nohria switched strategies and started investing massively in online content as well. One would think that with two star strategy professors on board in the likes of Christensen and Porter, HBS would have an easy time cruising through these challenges. However, it turns out, these professors disagree about the potential opportunity/threat that is posed by the Internet and thus do not see eye to eye about the best way to move forward.

Christensen's view is that about half of the universities in the U.S. could face bankruptcy within 15 years due to technology. According to him, HBS faces the same threat, as he does not see HBX as the solution to the disruption caused by the internet. "It should be cheap and simple," according to Christensen, which cannot be said about HBX. Porter, on the other hand, claims that HBS is doing the right thing by continuing to focus on its core brand and strengths and using the Internet – through HBX – to reach more customers while not directly competing with its own offline offerings.

If Christensen and Porter cannot agree[135], then it's definitely not up to me to take a stand as to who is right or wrong. What's sure though, is that the internet is about to change our educational model as we know it. Find out more about HBX online (where else?!?).

What is the real value of an MBA? And is it worth the cost?

An MBA is an expensive undertaking – and in the last couple of years, the cost of an MBA has only gone up. The budget for my two years at HBS was neatly published on the HBS website. It stated the fixed amounts I would have to pay to HBS as well as budgeted costs for other necessities such as housing and food[136]. And yes, these are YEARLY estimates for a two-year program!

---

135 Find some interesting articles on the subject here: **http://goo.gl/1gXuB7** and here: **http://goo.gl/MrX0iV**
136 These are class of 2014 values as published by HBS in the spring of 2012. Note that HBS publishes different budget numbers depending on your marital status, and if you have children. The budget figures here show the amounts for a single student. Find more recent estimates on the HBS MBA website.

135a

135b

HBS Fee	Tuition	$53,500
HBS Fee	Health Fee	$930
HBS Fee	Health Insurance Plan	$2,168
HBS Fee	Program Support Fee	$6,690
Living Costs	Room and Utilities	$10,800
Living Costs	Board, Personal, Other	$13,112
Total HBS Fees		$63,288
Total Living Costs		$23,912
TOTAL/year		$87,200

While the tuition and health costs are fixed and are represented accurately, I do have some doubts about the assumptions for housing and personal costs. There are a couple of things to be said about this. First of all, Cambridge is an expensive place to live. Demand for housing is way bigger than supply, making it pretty tricky to find affordable housing. Also, HBS budgets the cost of room and utilities based on paying rent 10 months of the year, as most students leave Boston for the summer months. And indeed, those living in the HBS dorms can sign a 10-month lease with HBS. But all the others living in HBS apartments or renting a place on the private market, have to pay rent for the summer months as well, which already drastically understates these rather conservative budget estimates.

Second, a lot of people forget about another important 'hidden cost' – NOT having an income for almost two years. If the average HBS student made about $50,000 a year[137] prior to school, that is an opportunity cost of $100,000. Third, the lifestyle at HBS and the cost of living in the U.S. can be expensive. Tickets for HBS parties can go for as much as $150 a person. On top of that, you need a tuxedo to go to some of these ($85 rental[138]) and the Mrs. needs a nice dress (let's say she rents it from Rent-The-Runway for another $150). Nicely dressed people need cabs to and from the party ($50). And the evening ends up costing somewhere between $500 and $600 a couple. Imagine doing this on a bi-weekly basis… And then there is all the

---

137 Which is probably a relatively low assumption.
138 I really would advise buying a tux though – a convenient and affordable place to do so is Keezer's, a 10-minute walk from campus. Check them out here: **http://goo.gl/Pc6AU9**

travel organized every other weekend to fill the gaps... For international students, there is the additional cost of flights home. Though to be fair, these expenses are not a mandatory part of the HBS program.

Costs aside, what is the value of the MBA? Most schools (including HBS) will publish the difference in salaries that their students make prior to post-grad school[139]. As such, they want to demonstrate the potential gains students get from going to their school. This raises some interesting questions. Is the value of an MBA to be measured by the job people get out of school? Is an MBA from an elite institution nothing more than an elaborate quality screening on intelligence and aptitude for a next employer? If so, is that really worth the cost described above?[140]

An MBA is expensive, and I do agree that the value of a lot of MBAs is questionable. However, an MBA should not only be about looking at monetary benefits. It is about the experience, making new friends, building a network, having new insights on life and work, becoming a better leader, being inspired by others and the environment, making a career switch, and maybe even finding one's partner for some. Hence, the decision to pursue an MBA should be more than just about a short-term cost/benefit analysis. For me, it was about the experience. It was about living abroad. It was about a relatively easy way of living in the U.S. for some time with my American girlfriend (without having to go through the hassle of getting a green card). It was about fulfilling my curiosity about Harvard and its educational principles. It was about spending time with some of the best and brightest. It was about making friends for life

---

139 Find some salary data of its graduates published by HBS here: **http://goo.gl/0v4mxY**

140 Though a bit dated, there is an interesting article in the New York Times that looked at some of the impact an MBA had on people's lives. Another interesting article comes from The Economist: "Trouble in the Middle". Find both articles here: **http://goo.gl/kHpVfB** and here: **http://goo.gl/QQhSFD**

139

140a

140b

from all over the world. It was about working for a toilet paper manufacturing company in Ghana. It was about experiencing all that and becoming a better professional in the process. And I might only be able to quantify the real cost/benefit of that many many many years from now.

70

Should MBA programs specialize? The case of some top MBA programs

Differentiation or targeting the masses – what should some of the top business schools do? Some schools already have a reputation going for them. If you want to get into finance, go to Wharton. If entrepreneurship is your thing, aim for Stanford. For general management skills, go HBS![141] And we all know what business school is considered the party school…

A. Stanford	○	○	1. General Management
B. INSEAD	○	○	2. Entrepreneurship
C. Wharton	○	○	3. Party
D. HBS	○	○	4. Finance

Connect the dots…

Going forward, should business schools try to strengthen their specialized reputations, or should they reinforce the image of being a school

---

141 These are general reputations linked to the schools that are familiar to most of the student body. The reputations that I describe here are the result of discussions I had with many (prospective and actual) MBA students and from reading online MBA content. These reputations are not communicated or reinforced by the schools in any way.

that fits all? HBS has long been criticized for being late in the tech-game compared to Stanford, for instance. Compared with MIT and Stanford, "we have, in a sense, less tech in the air," says HBS's Dean, Nitin Nohria, according to a Wall Street Journal article[142]. The article also states an important disadvantage that HBS has compared to these schools – where other faculties at MIT and Stanford are nearly integrated with the business schools, HBS is isolated from other Harvard faculties[143].

I personally believe each school should have a unique selling position. But I also think this edge might be even more important for schools that do not make the top 5 or top 10 business school rankings. They need to market themselves as the school for engineers, or the school for entrepreneurs or marketers. The top business schools can have a differentiating factor but should nevertheless focus on offering a program that is as well-rounded as possible.

I thus fully support HBS's engagement and investments to bring more tech and entrepreneurial vibes to the school. And while this is not something that can be quickly cultivated by opening an i-Lab on campus, I do believe that in time it will lead to a more conducive breeding ground for entrepreneurs within the walls of HBS. Focus on what's key, differentiate where necessary – I almost start sounding like a HBS Strategy Professor myself!

71

The MBA ranking – my personal way of ranking programs

Earlier in this book, I mentioned the importance of the MBA rankings. Right after graduating from HBS, some of the publications that make these rankings reached out to me. They sent me an email asking if I would be willing to

---

142 Should Harvard Business School Hit Refresh? Melissa Korn And Lindsay Gellman, Feb. 4, 2015. **http://goo.gl/K2UmUs**
143 As mentioned before, this might change soon. After receipt of a generous donation from alum John A. Paulson (M.B.A. '80) – $400 million, the largest donation ever made in Harvard's history – to support the school of Engineering and Applied Sciences, a new Engineering School will be built right in front of HBS!

participate in a survey to rate my HBS MBA experience. Of course I would! The questions were very diverse, and were very different from one survey to another. They included the topic of out-of-school salaries, how happy I felt with my academic and non-academic experience at HBS, the quality of the faculty, the job opportunities, etc. Most of these things seemed heavily correlated with what to expect of life AFTER school, but very little with life DURING school. With the typical U.S. MBA program being a 2-year endeavor (a long time for an average 26-year old!), I believe quality of life should be an aspect to consider for students when applying to schools. This quality of life can include things like local cost of living, crime rates, number of non-stop airline connections and cultural life of the city. But when reflecting on what really made me suffer during my two years in Boston, it was the long and cold Boston winter. The cold had been so hard on me that I decided to add the climate as a quality of life parameter in my own personally created MBA ranking!

So here's how I proceeded with this. First of all, when looking at MBA programs, students want to pursue an MBA at a reputable institution. So I took the top 5 schools of some of the most prominent MBA rankings online, including rankings from Forbes, the Economist, the FT, US News and Business Week[144]. Second, I limited my research to U.S. schools and

---

144 These rankings are readily available online – Sources for rankings:
Forbes: **http://goo.gl/xaQH64**
The Economist: **http://goo.gl/5U4Xy6**
FT: **http://goo.gl/oGUVJo**
US News: **http://goo.gl/VjZA46**
Businessweek: **http://goo.gl/swMcdl**

144a

144b

144c

144d

144e

filtered out non-U.S. schools. By now, I was left with 10 schools in 8 U.S. cities. Third, I decided to only cover the average temperatures during the months that students actually spend in those places, hence filtering out the months of June, July and August. Finally, I sorted the results from high to low. This allowed me to come up with my own MBA Performance and Weather Ranking[145].

In short and not surprisingly, Berkeley-Haas and Stanford top the weather ranking. Tuck seems to be the biggest victim of my approach and can be found at the bottom in place 10. Interestingly, I seemed to have developed a ranking system that gives Harvard its worst ranking across the board – number 7 overall, behind some other not-so-warm schools such as Columbia and Wharton. Now here is a real challenge for the HBS administration – get the weather right!

72

London School of Exploitation – time to question our schooling system?

LSE usually stands for the London School of Economics, but in the spring of 2015, its students were protesting what they call the London School of Exploitation. The LSE students were lobbying for cheaper tuition, better support for employees, and divestment from unethical businesses. While I never saw any protests like that at HBS, it made me reflect on some of the ethical issues related to our schooling system. Should an education like the one I got at Harvard Business School cost $126,000[146]? Is it OK for access to HBS to be skewed in favor of the 'elite'? Is it correct to have business schools teaching students how companies can make a lot of money by, for example, limiting their exposure to taxes? Should business schools continue to brag about how much their graduates make compared to what they

---

145 Find and overview of the above rankings at the time of writing as well as my very own weather ranking here: **http://goo.gl/Rv9mNh**
146 This does not only include tuition fees, but also some other costs such as healthcare coverage, etc.

made before school (and should their rankings be based on that)? And how is HBS addressing some of these issues as a thought leader?

First of all, HBS has invested massively in courses on ethics as part of the mandatory curriculum. On top of that, HBS collaborates with non-profits; through HBS sponsored fellowships, students can work for institutions that cannot necessarily afford an MBA grad as an employee. Third, HBS seems to be accepting more people with a background in non-profit organizations or organizations whose goals go beyond quarterly earnings alone. The one thing that I really found enlightening at HBS though, was one of my personal favorite elective classes in EC year – a class called "Re-inventing Capitalism".

The class (with the best name ever if you ask me) focuses on demonstrating that the hunt for profits can go hand in hand with an ecologic and ethical approach to business. We discussed cases of banks only investing in sustainable businesses and being successful by having this unique vision. We discussed companies devising programs to pull people out of poverty while ensuring corporate success by having a devoted workforce in return. But most of all, the class was about questioning our current way of behaving and conducting business – and how we, as future business leaders would want to change this. I believe this latter part is key: we should all understand our responsibility in some of the issues we see around us. Many of the tough questions asked in class do not have a satisfactory answer in today's world. We all have a role to play, and our schools are a platform we can leverage to study, develop and expand on potential solutions.

The future of the MBA program will be about more than accurately measuring the WACC[147] of companies or learning about optimal organizational design structures. The next generation MBAs will have much tougher issues to deal with: rising inequality, security, global warming, scarcity of resources, increasing instability, the next level of globalization, etc. The MBAs of the future will have to be more than just business leaders – they will have to step up to participate in shaping the society.

The one "Reinventing Capitalism" course at HBS that addresses these kind of issues is not enough to make that shift happen, nor is the occupy LSE movement providing the correct approach or messages to address

---

147 WACC = weighted average cost of capital – the cost of capital for firms.

very real problems. But I believe these little things are the start of a revolution, one which I hope we as leaders will manage proactively rather than reactively. One for which all of us hold a massive responsibility. And one for which I hope HBS can contribute by shaping the leaders of tomorrow.

PART
IX

THE HARVARD BRAND
AND ITS PERKS AND
DISADVANTAGES

73

John Harvard

Before diving into the perks and disadvantages associated with the Harvard brand, it is worth understanding the origins of the name 'Harvard'. Harvard University was named after John Harvard, an English Minister in America in the 17th century known for his love of learning. John Harvard is often considered the founding father of Harvard College. However, the school that carries his name today was founded three years before John Harvard donated a large part of his wealth and his library to the school on this deathbed. It was because of this gift that the school was renamed Harvard. Calling John the sole founder of Harvard would thus be giving him too much credit. His donation probably contributed to kick starting the school however. Should we see him as an early-day venture capitalist?

In Harvard Yard, a bronze statue can be found supposedly representing John Harvard. However, as there was no way to know what he looked like (the statue was erected late 19th century, almost 200 years after his death), the man pictured in the statue is an idealization of what a man like John Harvard was supposed to have looked like. Today, the statue is duly photographed by tourists, and it is believed that touching the tip of the left shoe of the statue brings luck. With hundreds of tourists rubbing John's left shoe tip on a daily basis in Harvard Yard, it is not surprising that a common joke amongst students is to pee on the statue's foot at night and watch tourists come in early the next morning to rub it… Seems like this might be a 'perk' to Harvard students, and a rather inconvenient unknown to the many visitors of the school…

74

The H-bomb

The name Harvard must be one of the most recognized brands in the educational space, and is associated with other things such as 'elite', 'intelligence', and 'money'. Name-dropping Harvard, also referred to as dropping the H-bomb, however, can be a double-edged sword.

On the one hand, being associated with the Harvard brand name opens a lot of doors. I have been impressed by the level of access I get to senior executives and politicians when looking for jobs or speakers for events. The Harvard name on my resume has led to my success applying for jobs I would otherwise not even have been considered for. People tend to think of Harvard grads as highly intelligent individuals... suits me! And, finally, I have been told that the H-bomb is particularly handy in the dating scene... On the other hand, being a 'Harvard boy' can also add pressure in the workplace. It seems as though some people make it a key goal to outsmart the Harvard people. Outside of work, the Harvard brand can also cause some jealous reactions. I vividly remember being put on the spot by an immigration officer at Boston airport. I had forgotten to enter a field on one of my immigration documents and the officer, noticing that I was entering the country on a Harvard-sponsored VISA, asked how it was possible that I was smart enough to get into Harvard but too dumb[148] to fill out an immigration document.

Hence, to avoid some of the controversy around the H-bomb, a lot of students and former students of the H-institution tend to say they 'studied in Boston' or 'went to school in Boston' when asked about their academic background. I would never drop the H-bomb instantly, but rather say I went to Harvard when people would specifically ask me where I did my MBA. Otherwise, when asked about my life, I would just say that I am originally from Belgium and moved to the U.S. to further my studies. This isn't because I am not proud of going to Harvard – on the contrary. Yet I don't want people to think of me as a Harvard product first, before they get to know

---

148 Yes, those were his exact words.

me. It is for that same reason that I am not strolling around in obvious Harvard clothing.

So, is the H-bomb a perk or a disadvantage? Well, let's not fool ourselves – it is a definite perk! And one I have come to enjoy through professional opportunities, meeting some of the most interesting people I have ever met, and if I would be more open about my association with Harvard, one I could probably use in the dating scene as well!

75

The business of business schools – does HBS lead the pack?

The MBA programs of different business schools are ranked by different kinds of publications. Some of the most renowned rankings include the ones from Forbes, US News and Businessweek. These publications typically use salary gains, surveys amongst students and recruiters, GMAT and GPA scores and average salaries post-MBA. But here's a thought – if a business school is about teaching students how to be 'successful in business', shouldn't we rate business schools on how well they are at doing business themselves? Shouldn't we have a look at their performance? Wouldn't that be the ultimate measure of success of a business school? Which program would top the 'B-school business model' ranking? Let's see what the data says.

In 2010, HBS recorded a revenue of $467 million. Almost half of this revenue came from tuition fees – Exec[149] and MBA. Nearly one third came from publishing. Another 24% was gathered through endowments and gifts. It's this last part that left me rather curious. About a fourth of HBS's yearly revenue depends on donations, raised through a thousand different funds established over the years by individual donors, corporations, and reunion classes.

---

149 Exec is short for HBS's Executive Education programs. These are programs offered to experienced professionals and are typically only a couple of weeks long. They tend to be very expensive and sponsored by companies.

Not surprisingly, the cost-base of HBS is headcount-driven. In 2010, 50% of operational expenses were linked to salaries, a bit over $200 million. Splitting this amount equally over the about 1000 FTEs (full-time equivalents) employed by HBS leaves each of these FTEs with an average yearly salary of $200,000. It's not the most statistically correct analysis to use in this case, but it's a quick and fun calculation to make.

With more than 50% of its revenue generated from sources unrelated to tuition, HBS Inc. has a great competitive advantage compared to some of its closest competitors. No other business school can even come close to some of HBS's publishing revenues or endowments. Based on available data, Stanford had a revenue of $155 million in 2011, a third compared to HBS. INSEAD received €6 million of donations in 2010. Moreover, historical trends show that the revenue base of HBS has experienced a sharp rise, with tuition income and endowments almost doubling between 2002 and 2010, and with a steadily growing income related to publishing in difficult times for the written word.

In summary, while one can question the MBA program rankings, it seems that HBS tops the list of best B-school business model. An important part of revenue comes from non-MBA sources such as publishing revenue and executive education programs. HBS is number 1! So HBS has the most money and seems to demonstrate it is the best at running a business itself! How can one choose not to go to this school!?!

76

Harv-art

The HBS campus has some pretty neat buildings and some of the interiors of these buildings are at least as inspiring as the lessons there. During my time at HBS, the walls of the buildings were decorated with (Harv-)art from the Schwartz collection. According to the HBS website, the goal of displaying this collection is to "inspire students to think creatively and incorporate art into their lives."

We owe this collection to Gerald Schwartz (HBS alum Class of 1970) who stated that "artistic presence was the only thing missing at HBS when I went there. I wanted to change that."[150] In 1995, Gerald Schwartz and a team from HBS began purchasing contemporary art for the HBS buildings most frequented by students. The results of this initiative can be admired on the HBS campus today.

I found some pieces of the collection to be inspiring indeed. Others were a bit more of a stretch to get my head around. It's a pleasure however to be surrounded by artistic pieces. I have often found some of our guests on the HBS campus be particularly impressed by some of the paintings hanging on our walls. But feel free to make up your own mind on the Schwartz collection here: **http://goo.gl/DfGcwx** or while visiting the HBS campus.

77

TGIFs – the early day introduction to the food sponsors

TGIF – Thank God/Goodness it's Friday! On a monthly basis, the HBS Student Association (SA) organizes a free drinks & snack activity on Spangler lawn. These TGIFs tend to be sponsored by a consultancy or investment bank. It's HBS's TGIF event – an ideal way to mingle with students from other sections and from other years.

The TGIFs were also a good introduction to what I came to call the 'consultancy banner'. The table with the sponsored drinks and snacks would be decorated with a banner featuring the name of a consultancy or other firm that was recruiting on campus. Little did I know at my first TGIF how common these banners would be during my time there.

Every conference, every club event, and the vast majority of social events that offered free refreshments suffered from banneritis – a proliferation of consulting company banners. The livelihood of these events all

---

150 As quoted from **http://goo.gl/lnspxc**, where an overview of the Schwartz collection can also be found.

depended on the generous contributions of firms. The same was true for the club of which I was President (the Belgian club of Harvard and MIT), where a banner would be provided by our sponsoring firms to showcase their brand while our members were enjoying the sponsored Pad Thai and crispy spring rolls. And it has to be said – our loyalty to these firms only went as far as their contributions, as we had three different consultancies sponsor our events during my two year window of being part of this club. But whether the food is sponsored by a company with a green, a red or a black logo, the Pad Thai tasted all the same to me!

Moreover, these firms are specifically eager to sponsor events (and TGIFs in the first place) that take place in the first few months of RC year. During that time, HBS installs a strict 'no recruitment activities' policy on campus to ensure that the freshly arrived MBA students can fully focus on getting a grip on the class workload and learning how to prepare cases. Events such as TGIF provided firms with a somewhat passive form of early entry on campus recruiting activities – or at least a way to have their name out there in the early days of the MBA. Clever marketing? Cheap brain-washing techniques? Or money poorly spent on their part? Well, I am sure those guys know what they are doing. After all, most of them probably hold MBAs themselves…

78

Recruiting perks

I didn't fully appreciate the ban on recruiting at the beginning of the semester of the first year at HBS until hell broke loose after the end of the recruitment ban period. After that my inbox was spammed by the AAAAAA, BBBBBB, CCCCCC,… consultants of this world.

As fall announces itself through cold nights and falling leaves, one can tell when recruiting season starts by the changing clothing habits of most students. The casual sweaters and loose t-shirts are replaced by suits and ties. Besides having your classmates dress up, recruiting season has another big advantage. On Monday, the XXXXXX investment fund served pizza for dinner. On Tuesday I was fed by the fancy YYYYYY investment bank buffet while Wednesday's menu was provided by a major overseas bank. On Thursday, the healthcare club at HBS organized an early Thanksgiving dinner for all its organizing members... sponsored by most of above mentioned companies and many many many more. One would almost forget that the real goal here is to get a job, and not getting fat!

The recruiting perks go far beyond free food and drinks though. Recruiting companies often fly students from Boston to their offices for interviews wherever they are located. I too had to make a couple of trips for recruiting purposes, though I was not part of the crew that purposely applied to jobs in say Los Angeles to score a free plane ticket to the West Coast (and why not stay a couple of extra days on the sunny West Coast while we are there, right?).

But it's only after the interviews are done that the real fun begins. After a successful interview for an internship with a major consultancy, I promptly received a box of exquisite (and expensive) chocolates in the mail, along with an invite to go on a complimentary trip to London for the weekend to get to know the company better. So that's how I ended up on an overnight flight to London to spend the weekend with other potential business school recruits for summer internships across that consultancy's European offices. The weekend was fun, full of entertaining activities, food and drinks. On a side note, more than half of us got sick on the last night of the weekend because of food poisoning. It's ironic how all the food sponsoring seemed to have turned against them at one point... But then again, can't quite blame the consultancy for what happened.

Upon accepting the offer just a couple of days after coming back from the London trip, I received another gift in the mail: a bottle of expensive champagne! What a great way to welcome someone to the company! I loved it!

Game on, recruiting perks! And yes, the weekend to London perk definitely stood out compared to the regular boring corporate PowerPoint presentation in Aldrich to advertise one's company.

79

Showing the love – SWAG

SWAG, short for 'Stuff We All Get', refers to promotional items organizations or companies give to promote their brand(s). At HBS, one will encounter all kinds of SWAG, with the most common SWAG being associated to HBS and Harvard! Stores in Harvard Square are full of it!

Another common type of SWAG is called 'recruiting SWAG', coming from a multitude of companies. I have a collection of pens, water bottles and shirts from dozens of organizations. The most useful item I got was an umbrella – which comes in very handy in Boston!

Then there is 'group feeling' SWAG. This can range from section SWAG (we got customized sunglasses and even our own section M&Ms), SWAG linked to the different clubs at HBS, and the nifty graduation SWAG.

Last but not least, there is the 'perform well in class' SWAG. This category is the toughest one to get your hands on, as it is given by professors as a reward for exceptional class performance on a certain case in class. In this category, we find items such as the 'best negotiator' T-shirt from our Negotiations class. We have a Captain's hat award for the person winning the overfishing simulation exercise (I got this prize by the way!) and there is the famous baseball hat for the Masters of our accounting class simulation. This kind of SWAG is a gift from the Professor body at HBS to reward those who perform well on their beloved simulation exercises. Ahoy Captain SWAG!

80

Fancy HBS parties – the HBS party location hunt

With a student body of 900+ a year, organizing school-wide dinner and dance events is not a straightforward task. Yet these events exist – and the organizers have found a selection of key venues that can cope with both the capacity requirements and the relatively high quality standards of the average HBS folks. Here are some of the HBS-wide parties and their traditional hosts:

The MBA opening party for RCs – venue: courthouse in Boston

Organized by the Student Association (SA), the MBA opening party is the first major party at HBS to which all of the freshly started first year students were invited. The party involves music, dancing, gambling (with fake money) and enjoying the view from the courthouse. With the courthouse being built on the waterfront, and with the construction facing the water being made entirely out of glass, the views over the Boston Harbor area were nothing short of spectacular.

My rating: location 10/10, fun-factor 9/10, organization 9/10, value for money 10/10 (it's free! Very rare for a HBS party!)

The end of RC year celebration – venue: a castle in Newport

Once a year, the cute beach town of Newport, Rhode Island, gets to witness the arrival of 900+ HBS MBA students. Every year around March/April, the local castle is transformed into a huge drinking/dining/dancing venue for the students. To be able to host this amount of people, the rooms in the castle are extended by several (luxury) tents. School buses drive students back and forth from local hotels to the castle. The food is served buffet style (and was mostly cold by the time I got to it). Music was great though. And it's fun to see everyone dressed up in nice tuxedos and gala dresses. However, it turned out to be a very expensive trip.

But there is also more to the weekend than just the event in the castle. Most sections will organize another event the day after the party – my section organized a full-blown lobster bake! Moreover, it is worth taking a stroll through the adorable little city center of Newport. My personal rating: location 7/10, fun-factor 8/10, organization 8/10, value for money 5/10

The Christmas party – venue: the Boston Westin hotel

More of a traditional hotel location with hotel food and hotel atmosphere. Great fun as the group of 900 students breaks up into their respective sections to do some section celebration SkyDeck-style!

My personal rating: location 5/10, fun-factor 8/10, organization 8/10, value for money 7/10

The EC gala – venue: Top of the Hub at Prudential Tower

Imagine having a walking dinner/party on the top floor of the tallest building of Boston. Food and drinks were included in the price, the music was great, and the view of the city was nothing less than astonishing! Hundreds of other soon-to-graduate MBAs mingled in their nicest gala clothes. Welcome to the HBS EC graduation party! I really enjoyed this party – and also realized that I might not see the majority of the people in that room ever again in my life. We had been sharing the same campus, the same party venues, and the same cases for the last two years. At our graduation party, we would be sharing a lot of these things for the last time. When admiring the view over Boston from the Top of the Hub, I could also spot the Courthouse building in the distance – the place where it all began less than two years earlier…

My personal rating: location 10/10, fun-factor 9/10, organization 9/10, value for money 8/10

81

The Entrepreneurial and Venture Capital Treks… Will the next Steve Jobs please stand up!

HBS's entrepreneurial treks bring students at HBS in contact with the entrepreneurial world. The treks are organized in different locations, from Boston to New York and San Francisco. During most treks, students visit start-ups, venture capital firms[151], and firms offering support services tailored for start-ups. They are a great avenue for students to get a feel for

---

151 These are firms investing in (often small or young) companies and start-ups. They tend to make several bets on different companies and hope to (massively) cash out on a couple of them when these firms grow substantially or when they end up going public.

how startups work, the pain entrepreneurs go through, and the opportunities they are hunting for. It also offers a different perspective on the business world compared to visiting the corporate offices of consultancy firms and/or multinational organizations. The huge glass buildings and fancy offices are now replaced by small hidden offices, often messy and utterly crowded. It is great to have those (often young) entrepreneurs to share experiences.

I participated in two of those treks in Boston. The first one, organized by the HBS Entrepreneurship Club, took us to a number of young startups in the Boston area. Boston has become home to a surprisingly growing number of startups in recent years. The Boston trek I participated in was just a one-day event – treks organized in more distant locations (New York or the West Coast) often stretch over two or three days. The first company on the list that we visited was ABC[152] – a company that matches people looking for custom-made items with people or companies that can produce them (think a fancy wooden table that you want to look a certain way). The office was not exactly much of an … office. It looked like an old warehouse that had been transformed into some office-like space. The paint was peeling off the walls and the furniture was mismatched.

The CEO of the company – cool guy, loose jeans, wild hair (at least what was left of it) showed us around and presented us to his staff members scattered around the … eh … office. Afterwards, he took us to a meeting room where a member of his team would tell us a bit more about what they did and how they did it. While I wasn't very impressed by the office (coming from the corporate world myself), I was impressed with the energy in that building. Everyone was full of it! People looked relaxed yet driven – cool yet professional. I was impressed by ABC's culture – and by the brilliance of their CEO. While he didn't say all that much, every comment he made was enlightening – a combination of cleverness and surprising honesty.

Second on the list was DEF, a startup providing companies with an overview of bugs and issues with their apps (and other software). The founder and CEO was a young guy, and from the looks of their office, they had just raised a lot of money from venture capital firms. He told me about the little

---

152 Names of the companies visited have been changed for privacy reasons.

apartment they had rented initially, in which they were cramped together, fighting for space. The office they had now was a fancy Cambridge office on the XXth floor of a glass and concrete building. Yet the CEO was still very humble and open in his presentation to us.

The final company on the list worth mentioning was GHI. What struck me most about this company was the very different dynamic. Employees in that company behaved as if they were corporate employees, which was probably due to the fact that the CEO had an ego closer to that of a corporate CEO than that of the other entrepreneurs we had met earlier that day. The office looked worn down and was poorly lit. The sum of the visits that day made it into an interesting experience; we got to meet very different entrepreneurs in different stages of business success and with different ways of building their future empire. And all that within a two square mile area in Cambridge!

The second trek I participated in at Boston was of a very different kind, yet it still very much linked to the entrepreneurial world. It was a trek organized by the venture capital (VC) club at HBS and it took us to a couple of VC firms. This time, we were hosted in fancy buildings fully made out of glass, where every single meeting room provided a great view over the city. While interesting, the VC trek was less my cup of tea – I much preferred the entrepreneurial trek a few weeks earlier. It left me wondering though how people from these very different worlds (the entrepreneurs wearing loose jeans in the warehouse-like offices and the VC people in nice ties strolling around their fancy offices) could work together so efficiently to build successful new ventures. Listening to some of the success stories presented by the venture capital firms during their PowerPoint presentations proved me wrong – a lot of interesting companies were built by bringing together the best of these two worlds! I guess money can close a lot of cultural gaps.

82

HBS spotting...

There are many other smaller yet important perks to HBS. First, there is the fact that one can show their love for HBS in very interesting ways – going as far as having a license plate of one's Porsche fully HBS customized (a student spotted a Porsche with the license plate HBS4MBA in California – a picture of it was duly shared on Facebook). HBS faculty and staff enjoy other perks, as Dean Nohria clearly demonstrated by showing up on live nationwide TV during the Super Bowl sitting next to Michael Douglas[153] (the moment was shared on Facebook yet again). Third, there are the perks related to getting invited to some interesting events that one would otherwise struggle to get invited to. As an example, I received an invitation for a black tie event organized by the Belgian embassy in New York. Finally, there is the perk of having access to some of HBS's international assets. Indeed, HBS has club houses all over the world where alumni and staff alike come together for events and other exchanges. Even in Boston, there's some perks associated to being affiliated to HBS – how about going for a fancy Sunday brunch in the HBS faculty club house?

---

153 A famous actor.

PART

X

DON'T FORGET – IT'S ALL ABOUT GETTING A JOB...

83

Offline recruiting resources – CPD

When searching my HBS calendar for the acronym CPD, I instantly found 66 hits – and these are only the activities I signed up for! CPD is short for Career and Professional Development and is the branding used for most recruiting activities managed by HBS. Preparing students to find a job out there is a key priority for HBS; and CPD is their way of doing so.

There are all kinds of CPD activities. In my early MBA days, there were the CPD orientation days ("To learn about the vast array of programs offered to support your career development"), the CPD super days ("Discovering your career vision") and the CPD Career vision days ("Realize your career vision, develop your job search strategy and advance your knowledge through industry education").

Those latter events were by far the most interesting. Facilitated by Tim Butler, Director of Career Development at HBS, the sessions focused on finding your best potential job fit. The two years at HBS are about more than cases and simulations, they are also a period of reflecting on your future career. The CPD career vision day was the start of that process, and we did so using Tim Butler's 100 jobs exercise[154]. After a short introduction to his methodology, Tim Butler provided each student with a list of 100 jobs. The jobs ranged from actor to accountant. Within a couple of minutes, each student had to personally select their top-10 jobs that they would love doing and rank them in order from 1 to 10, where 1 was their preferred job.

The following day, students met up in small pre-defined groups of four to five to discuss the jobs they had selected. These groups were facilitated by EC students[155] and had the objective of identifying common themes amongst the jobs. For example, someone who chose the jobs of actor, politician and CEO, might have a theme going in the direction of "likes being the center of attention" and "enjoys public speaking". These themes were then

---

154 For more information, read Tim Butler's book "Getting Unstuck"
155 EC is short for Elective Curriculum – it refers to second year MBA students.

narrowed down to a couple of key themes that would eventually boil down to some types of jobs that could be a good fit. Students going through this exercise had their trained EC facilitator and their RC peers to support and help them throughout by questioning and sharing observations.

In the days and weeks after the exercise, students were able to discuss their results with other members of the CPD organization. They can help analyze some of the themes that have come out of the 100 jobs exercise, and confirm these trends with data they got from a personality test that students had to complete online.

This CPD exercise based on Tim Butler's Career Leader approach is not mandatory – yet about 60-70% of students seem to sign up for it every year – and so did I. I found the exercise interesting, though I didn't really get as much out of it as I wanted or had hoped for. For some, finding out what really makes them tick seems easy. For me, it has been a struggle for as long as I can remember. Still, I would recommend this exercise – it's a small investment of time and energy into getting to know a side of yourself you may not have been aware of! Later on in the year, the CPD activities continue to be omnipresent. The offering ranges from mock-interviews to prepare for recruiting season to having personal coaches guide you through the tough career choices. Then there are the more specific events ("Successful Career Switching"), the very specific events ("Intro to the U.S. Job Search for International Students") and the extremely specific events ("Business of Sports"). Some sessions involve working in small groups or 1-to-1, others are organized in the form of panel discussions.

I took advantage of some of the CPD offerings (It's all free by the way). I even signed up for a 1-to-1 coaching session with Tim Butler himself. Besides that, I had a personal coach that I met up with on 4-5 occasions to discuss job applications and job offers. I also had my share of mock-interviews and attended some of the panel discussions.

The conducive recruiting support at HBS is pretty vast and solid. The available resources are impressive. Yet I do believe that it is at least equally important (if not more so) for students to look for mentors and advisors outside of the HBS network – people that are not being paid to do so. These people could be former bosses or colleagues, family or friends, or peers at

HBS. Overall, having the combination of the professional HBS resources and a strong personal network is a solid basis to make further career decisions.

84

Online recruiting resources

Besides all the offline help, HBS has an online platform to facilitate job searching. The CPD platform offers a lot of resources. It is the platform on which you can make appointments with career coaches, where you sign up for on-campus recruiting events and – most importantly – where companies post the jobs they are looking to fill for summer internships and/or full-time positions. It is a huge online database in which students can look for opportunities by filtering location, industry, and a whole set of other parameters.

There are literally thousands of jobs posted there, ranging from jobs with well-known established firms to opportunities with smaller players and startup companies. All of the jobs listed have a detailed description of the function and the company, and have a link where interested students can upload their resume and motivation letter.

Applying for jobs is more time and energy consuming than I could ever have imagined. First, there's the part where you need to plough through the thousands of jobs to find the ones of interest to you. Second, there's no 'one-size-fits-all'-approach when it comes to preparing resumes and letters of motivation. Each application requires a customized approach to be in line with the job requirements. Third, there is the careful management of meeting the deadlines for job applications, with most jobs having different deadlines spread out over a period of a month or two.

Once all applications are in, the next milestone is waiting for an invite to an interview. These confirmations are provided in the CPD tool. If you get a confirmed status, you can sign up for one of the predetermined interview time-slots. Then there are the applications with a WAIT status – indicating that you did not make the initial shortlist, but that you might be contacted for an interview should others bail out. Finally, there's the fail status – you have not been selected to interview for that job. Or are you? Interestingly, HBS has a system that allows you to bid for interviews for jobs that you were not initially selected for, or for which you did not apply to for whatever reason. Every student gets allocated 1000 points in the CPD online system that can be freely distributed across a couple of jobs that they really want to interview for. Students get about a week or so to place their bids after most interview slots have been allocated. If they are the highest bidder in terms of points for additional interview spots, they will get an invite regardless of whether they applied or not, or if they had been turned down based on their resume or not.

I found this a very weird. Why would a company even want to interview someone that was not selected based on their resume or letter of motivation? What is the value of this bidding system to them? Has this system really resulted in some matches? I frankly have no idea, but I believe this to be a very odd approach to finding a job. My curiosity led me to try it, and it did get me an interview with an organization I hadn't applied to. They even ended up offering me an internship, which I turned down eventually.

At the end of the day, the online CPD resources are where a lot of the job hunting starts[156]. And once you have a couple of interviews lined up, things get serious. Then it's time to get back to the offline world – get those nice interview clothes out of the closet, people!

85

Going offline for the interview – the art of herding the HBS cattle

After a couple of months of CPD activities and company sponsored recruiting events, the month of January during the first year at HBS is when things

---

156 I am referring specifically to those who are looking at the HBS tools to find a job. Many members of the student body organize their job hunt all by themselves through personal or other connections.

start becoming really serious with regard to recruiting, finding internships and jobs. Until now, it was companies advertising themselves to students by offering information sessions, free food, drinks and tons of goodies. By January the tables have turned, as students are trying to secure an interesting internship at one of the top companies by going through a couple of intense interviewing days.

As could be expected, HBS provides a setting for recruiters and students to meet. Two hotels in Harvard Square are transformed into temporary recruiting centers. Students gather in hotel lounges, reading through their resumes one last time, awaiting to meet their future employers. Then, when the time has come, they will head to one of the hotel rooms[157] and wait for their turn to be interviewed, knowing that the next 30 minutes will heavily influence the rest of their professional lives.

Upon arrival at the Double Tree hotel, I was astonished to find hundreds of students scattered around, all of them Harvard MBAs, nicely dressed up in their dark suits. I couldn't help thinking that at least I had my European-style light grey suit with white pinstripes to stand out. But just like all the others, I would sit on a chair in front of a hotel room waiting for my interviewer to question me to pieces. As I sat on my chair looking at the HBS cattle moving around, I couldn't help questioning the irony of the process: the world's youngest and brightest business talents gathered in this hotel like cattle looking for a path to conquer the (business) world.

Not all companies conduct their interviews this close to campus though. A lot of other companies fly students to their respective headquarters or recruiting locations. Even most of those recruiting in the Double Tree hotel see this as an exercise to shortlist students and will follow-up later with interviews in their home bases. After my initial set of on-campus interviews for a summer internship, I was invited for a set of second round interviews in New York, Chicago, and Seattle.

The craziness of recruiting was very taxing on me. It is stressful, comes on top of our schoolwork and can feel really intense when trying to stand

---

157 Yes, most interviews are held in the hotel rooms. Rooms are equipped with a table with two chairs where the magic happens. A third chair is put in front of the hotel room to provide the students with a seat while they wait for their turn.

out amidst this crowd of smart and highly skilled individuals. The more determined and organized students have dozens of interviews lined up with all different companies, while claiming their love and passion for each of these companies. Competition is fierce amongst students in search of their beloved summer internship or job.

But maybe the real challenge is not with the students, but with the dozens of professionals at the other side of the interviewing table. Good luck to you, recruiters. Good luck finding the 'pearls' amongst the cattle.

Summer internships

The summer at HBS between the first and second year of the MBA program can almost be considered an integral part of the HBS curriculum. While students are officially on holiday for close to three months, the vast majority of them use these free months (June-July-August) to test their newly acquired knowledge in all kinds of business environments and cultures. It is also the time to reap the results of weeks and months of recruiting activities, networking, and interviews.

I pushed my summer internship experience to the extreme by interning for two different companies on two different continents. I spent the first six weeks of the summer interning at a management consulting firm in Europe, before moving to Japan for another seven-week internship assignment, this time for a local e-commerce business based in Tokyo. At the end of my MBA summer, I had lived/worked on four different continents over a period of only six months. This included my MBA in the U.S., my consultancy internship in Europe, my e-commerce internship in Asia and an earlier assignment as part of the FIELD3 program at HBS in Ghana, Africa! Pretty crazy thinking about it. Too bad I still missed out on Australia and Antarctica...

While intense, my summer was the best! Just three days after my final exam in Boston, I started working for a management consultancy in Brussels, Belgium. My first couple of days on the job were spent on training at their office in Milan. I would spend the majority of the day in trainings on the fundamentals of consulting – at night I would network with fellow interns from other European offices of the firm. These interns would all be in the midst of an MBA program at other business schools, think the likes of Wharton and INSEAD. Most of the training in Milan however was about how to enjoy really nice food on a piazza in Milan like real Italians do.

Once back in the Brussels office, the real work started. I would spend the next 5-6 weeks working on the redesign of the organization of a non-profit – something the consultancy does on a pro bono basis. I loved the project I was working on and the impact we had. I was really happy with most of the people I got to work with. Plus I adored the size of the paycheck I was getting. But I also realized that, while the experience was fantastic, the job of a management consultant was not what I saw myself doing. I didn't like the continuous intensity of the job, or the highly competitive culture (even between team members) that existed, or the fact that we would only be with an organization for a very short time span. I was very happy with my experience as a management consultant, only to realize that it was just not for me.

At the end of my consultancy project, and after recruiting fresh MBAs for future internships on a cool flying[158] event, I flew to Oslo, Norway to attend my brother's wedding. The day after he got married, I stepped on a plane to Tokyo, Japan, where I would spend the remaining seven weeks of my summer period working for Rakuten, an e-commerce company and key rival for Amazon in Asia and beyond.

It was on my first day at HBS that I was introduced to Rakuten. At the opening ceremony of the MBA program, Dean Nohria presented the alumni award to three alums who had achieved great things (or had done something that made them stand out). One of the alums honored on stage that day was Hiroshi Mikitani, co-founder and CEO of Rakuten. Rakuten, founded in 1997, is a $5 billion company today. While I had never heard of the company before, I was impressed by the story of this company and by Mikitani's personality. Little did I know then that I would work for his company one day as an intern or that, upon accepting their offer, I would have the

---

158 We flew ultralight-planes! Great way to attract new talent to the organization! Consultancies know how to organize recruiting events!!!

opportunity to have an impromptu dinner with him and a couple of other HBS MBAs in Boston. It was just us and Mr. Mikitani, having a steak in downtown Boston. Another Harvard perk I guess....

I was able to get a job at Rakuten as part of their 'Englishnization' program. Mikitani, who has global ambitions for his Japanese firm, wanted to instill a culture in his company that is closer to the western/American way of doing business. This is in sharp contrast to the Japanese way of working, built on respect for authority and hierarchy. To achieve this, he launched the Englishnization[159] program with the goal to have everyone in his company speak English. He believes that the aspects of the Japanese language itself enforce the culture of strict hierarchy he so wants to see evolve. Another part of his Englishnization program is to attract talent from outside of Japan – that's how I came into play.

I loved my time at Rakuten. I got to experience firsthand what it means to work for a Japanese company. It is about working long hours, going for drinks with colleagues and the boss right after work and ending up in a karaoke bar until the early hours of the (next) day. It is also about getting lost in translation, admiring the devotion of Rakuten's staff to their job, eye for detail and quality they have in everything they do. It was also about waiting in line every morning in front of the elevators that couldn't cope with the massive influx of people, often cramped by the hundreds in the small Tokyo offices. But I loved the whole experience and the can-do mentality at the company.

I was also amused by some interesting quirks in the way they managed their business. First of all, people could only get promoted if they managed to achieve a predetermined score on their English language test. Another thing that stood out to me was the reporting of some of their success indicators – I remember teams having to report on progress of sales for instance. Full Year target: 5000. Year-to-date achievement: 68. Every week, their year-to-date achievement would go up by a dozen or so. But their seemingly unreachable target of 5000 remained and had to stay visible throughout.

I loved my experience at Rakuten. It left me with an invaluable international experience in Japan, with some important background on the

159 Read all about it in Mikitani's book "MarketPlace 3.0"

evolutions in the e-commerce space, and with an interesting exposure to the entrepreneurial spirit that is still raging through this now corporate-sized organization.

When looking for internships, everyone has their own goals they want to pursue. My goals were simple. First, I wanted to be able to spend some time at home with friends and family in Brussels (where I ended up doing my consultancy internship). Second, I wanted to experience something outside of the pharmaceutical industry I had been working in for years prior to HBS (check!). Third, I wanted to have an additional international experience (check check!). My summer ended up fulfilling all of my requirements – I was lucky enough to have everything work out the way I wanted. Overall, my choices were very location and industry driven. Others might have had very different requirements than I did. Some would only settle for a job in banking in New York City as preparation for a future career in that industry. For others, the paycheck would be the most important thing. Finally, there are those that would want to jump into an entrepreneurial environment, wherever the job was located and whatever the paycheck. That's a personal choice each one has to make for themselves.

My summer was great, and I would recommend to all to spend as much time as possible working over the summer, ideally combining more than one internship. The internships are a unique and amazing experience and way to get to know a company, an industry, and a country. And one thing is for sure: at the start of my second year at HBS, my fellow students and I were full of stories of travels and jobs accomplished from all over the world. Work on, students!

87

The consulting and investment banking jobs...

Of all the different companies and industries recruiting on campus, two industries stand out. They are the management consultancy companies and the investment banks. They are similar in that they aggressively recruit

at the top business schools. They do so by hosting lots of on-campus recruiting events, spending a disproportionate amount on recruiting goodies
and are relatively aggressive in getting their brand name out to as many
students as possible through mailings and sponsoring. With 55% of HBS
students in my class ending up working in those two industries, the efforts
of those firms seem ever so effective. Still, competition between them to
attract the top talents is fierce.

I experienced both the management consultancy recruitment track as
well as the investment banking one – they were both very interesting yet
very different experiences. When recruiting for a management consultancy
role, it's all about solving business cases. Each interview consists of one
or more business cases that students need to crack. These cases can be
very different from one another. I had to come up with a strategy for a local
airline, then had to advise on a growth strategy for an industrial cleaning
company before deciding on the benefits of merging two key players in the
chemicals industry. There is an abundance of material put at the disposal
of students to learn how to crack those cases (not in the least by the consultancy firms themselves on their websites).

There are three key things to take into account when trying to apply
successfully to a consultancy firm. First, whatever happens, act confi-
dently. Second, allow yourself to be challenged and even allow yourself to
change your mind during the case exercise, but always do so by explaining
the different steps in your thinking that led you to do so. Say everything you
think out loud; the purpose of these kind of interviews is for them to understand your thought process. That is more important than the final outcome
of your reasoning. Finally, end by stating key messages like: "The customer
has to do this because of X, Y and Z." At the end of the day, that resembles
the output most consultancies produce for their clients.

Applying for a role in an investment bank is a whole different game. The
focus here lies in understanding financial results of companies and uncov-
ering investment opportunities. Some banks will ask you about some recent developments that have been mentioned in the media (e.g. mergers,

takeovers, and IPOs[160]) and what your thoughts are on them. But most of all, it's about pitching stocks. The most common questions asked during those interviews are of the likes of "What company stock should I invest in and why?" And applicants, be aware. This requires a lot of preparation. I had prepared three stocks to pitch for these interviews, only to find that at one of the interviews I was asked to pitch four stocks (this is where I had to improvise). When pitching stocks, it is important to understand the financials of the company, but even more so to be able to understand their business model and why you think that business model will be successful and hence lucrative to invest in going forward (and why other people have not discovered that yet).

After a first set of on-campus interviews, investment banks like to invite students to their headquarters for what they call the recruiting Super Days. This is where you will have to compete with talent from all over the world. Typically, applicants will go from one interview to the next during a Super Day, completing somewhere between five to eight interviews on one single day. Some interviewers focus on qualitative skills, others on financial skills, but most of them just want to hear you pitch a stock or a deal. So come prepared!

With all the recruiting going on, and with most of these Super Days being organized on weekdays, students end up missing several days of class flying around from headquarter to headquarter. HBS has a strict policy when it comes to class attendance – no unexcused absence will be allowed. Recruiting is not considered an excused absence[161]. However, most professors will allow one missed class per course for recruiting related reasons. But then again, what really matters here – having good grades at school or leaving school with a good job?

---

160   IPO stands for "Initial Public Offering" and refers to the first time a firm goes public, i.e. sells its stock to the public.
161   Examples of excused absences include illness, weddings or funerals of close family members. Any class absence needs to be submitted through an online platform.

88

Recruiting hell – those who struggle to make it…

Recruiting when in business school is as much about strategy as it is about doing well in interviews. Meet John, who desperately wants to start a career in investment banking at one of the top institutions. He applied to his personal top 5, made it to the last round of a couple of them, only to find out that he didn't end up getting any offers. By that time though, most of the second-tier banks (that hadn't made it to this personal shortlist) had finalized recruiting. John was left considering applying to smaller lower-tier banks or looking for another industry altogether.

Meet Tom. Tom is a great guy, and has a very clear idea of what he wants to do. He wants to go into private equity and has applied to every firm under the sun recruiting. But private equity is very competitive, and Tom did not have a job yet upon graduating.

Meet Mila. She thinks her dream is to go into management consulting, but she quickly realizes during the interviews that it doesn't seem to be a good fit. Mila is a smart woman, but she doesn't make it past the first round of any of her interviews. After further reflection, she decides that what she really wants is to work for a small entrepreneurial company. Halfway through recruiting season, she totally changes course and starts applying to a very different set of companies.

Getting things right from the start, and having a plan B and C is crucial during recruiting season. The competition is fierce, the number of spots limited, and the deadlines are unforgiving. Be prepared for the job you really want, and for the worst. Your Harvard MBA only gets you so far – having the right strategy and plans B and C in place are crucial!

89

HBS as a job creator

HBS is looking to employ some of its own freshly graduating MBAs as well! And it does so in different ways. The most common jobs for which HBS looks to recruit its own MBA talent is the management of its HBS fund, worth a couple of dozen million dollars. HBS also recruits for some of its own internal needs, like positions that support projects such as HBX[162]. Besides the HBS fund and HBX-like roles, HBS sponsors fellowships in different organizations to which HBS commits to pay half of the salary of the MBA (in most cases, students would be paid $100,000 a year, of which $50,000 is paid for by HBS). This allows smaller organizations and non-profits to attract a talented HBS MBA while being able to offer the student a competitive salary. The HBS fellowship fund sponsors organizations in all kinds of settings, from education to healthcare and research. Most fellowships only last for a year though.

I believe there are some unique functions as part of the fellowships. This is a good opportunity for some, and enriching that HBS is supporting these activities and organizations.

90

My own recruiting path – back to where I came from...

I already described where my recruiting activities landed me for my summer internships – I ended up working as a consultant in Europe for six weeks and with an e-commerce company in Japan for two months. But where did I end up after school?

Well, I didn't end up going down the path of management consulting – I just felt it wasn't my cup of tea. I didn't end up signing a contract with the Japanese company I had worked for over the summer either.

162 HBX is HBS's online educational offering – find out more here: **http://goo.gl/jLNktV**

I applied for different jobs, mainly for big corporations, and had a couple of offers I seriously considered. But eventually, I ended up accepting an offer from the company I had worked for prior to my HBS MBA. I went back 'home' – or not quite? Well, I did go back to the same company, but applied for and got a job in a different part of the organization and on a different continent. On August 1st 2014, almost two months after graduating from HBS, I started working as a Finance Director for the commercial organization in the Singapore office.

As I went back to my old love, was it worth going through the whole HBS MBA experience? Well, first of all, I did get a promotion and a salary increase. Also, my old love had partly sponsored my HBS endeavor (which I would have to reimburse if not staying with the company for at least three years). Second, the position they offered me was by far the most senior position I was offered by any of the corporations I had successfully applied to. As an older HBS MBA student, I was sometimes a bit frustrated that most of the corporate roles offered to MBA grads tended to be rather junior roles. Third, I think that measuring the MBA impact purely on its short-term benefits is extremely short-sighted. I will look back and try to value my MBA experience in 10 to 20 years from now and see what it really brought me. I will ensure to look beyond financial value and return on investment. I hope the MBA has made me worldlier and wiser person. I hope it will have left me with some friends for life. I hope it will help me with future challenges in my career. I hope the HBS network will help me to excel. And I believe that being a Finance Director in Singapore is a first step in that direction.

91

Spread the seed! Where do HBS students end up in the world? And are they rich?

HBS added an interesting page to its website in which they share detailed information on their recent alumni. The information provided shows the geographic location of where the students ended up living/working post graduation. It has salary data. And it also shows a distribution of the industries that students end up working in.

Some of the data was surprising to me. First of all, 84% of the students of the class of 2014 ended up staying in the U.S. 84%! Only 6% went to Europe, of which the bulk went to the UK (5%) and the remainder scattered within continental Europe (1%). This leaves about 10% of students going to other parts of the world, with 5% ending up in Asia and the rest spread out over Africa, the Middle East, Latin America and Canada. With about 34% of students in my class deemed international, the number of students that stayed in the U.S. seems very high[163]. When compared to a non-U.S. top business school such as INSEAD, the seed seems to be spread much more internationally. 45% ends up in Europe, 27% are attracted to Asia Pacific, followed by 11% of students going to North America.

55% of my former classmates work in finance or consulting today. The median base salary of my class is $125,000. 50% of students make between $110,000 and $135,000 a year right out of school. Surprisingly, the ones making the most money are the ones based in Europe, though this is probably since most students working in Europe are in the finance industry in London and can also be explained by the low dollar value compared to the Pound at the time of publication of the statistics. When comparing with INSEAD again, 51% goes into consulting or finance, close to the HBS figures[164].

All things considered, does a HBS MBA fulfill the myth of leading to a high-paying job and to a successful career? Well, we already addressed the range of salaries students right out of school are landing, which is one measure of success. Another measure would be to look at how older generations of HBS are doing. According to an article of PoetsAndQuants[165], Harvard Business School's MBAs are the highest earners in the 20-year period out of school of all MBAs. With a median 20-year income of

---

163 I debated on how international the school body of HBS really is in other parts of this book already.
164 Judge for yourself – find the HBS numbers here: **http://goo.gl/4c0hb3**
165 **http://goo.gl/Wt8El6**

164

165

$3,233,000 Harvard MBAs top the list above Stanford MBAs ($3,011,000) and Wharton MBAs ($2,989,000). These incomes might be understated, as according to the article, they do not include "stock-based compensation of any kind, the cash value of retirement benefits, or other non-cash benefits, such as healthcare."

However, these numbers have to be put into context. First of all, these are median values, and don't give a clear indication of the spread of the earnings among students. Second, a lot of benefits are not included, as mentioned above. And third, how are entrepreneurs considered if they may not have a fixed income but hold a substantial amount of value in stocks or other financial means? Whatever the shortcomings, there seems to be a correlation between earnings and rankings of MBA programs – and HBS seems to be topping (most of) the lists in both!

PART

XI

DON'T FORGET – IT'S
ALL ABOUT GETTING
A PARTNER...

92

Dating life at HBS (and surroundings)

Ah, the HBS dating life. As I was in a relationship throughout my period at HBS, I can only report on what I have observed of the dating life there. Hence, I asked some of my single friends at HBS about their thoughts and impressions of the HBS dating life. But let's start off here with my own observations first.

The Stone Age

With the Stone Age, I am not referring to the prehistoric era in our history. I am referring to the period at HBS where the fingers of a lot of women are being decorated with some impressive stones. There tends to be a huge wave of engagements during the 2-year HBS period, and that would become ever more visible through the shiny fingers of HBS women. I guess it's ever more obvious that the average HBS woman would not settle for an average ring?

Conquering the World

I remember a chat I had with a section-mate during my first few days at HBS. We were having a drink at the TGIF on Friday afternoon and were discussing women (as men tend to do). He had a clear priority for his time at HBS with regard to women – it was all about conquering the world, i.e. checking off as many countries on his list as possible… and he did not mean by actually visiting those countries. I guess that HBS, and more specifically Cambridge as a whole, is a pretty good place indeed to do so, with people from all over the world living together within just a square mile!

Post-Thanksgiving Couples

Ah, Thanksgiving will never be the same for me again. Students at HBS tend to get a couple of days off for this holiday and most will travel home to celebrate with friends, family and a partner they left behind. All too often, people travel back home for Thanksgiving for the first time since the start of their time at HBS. The experiences they went through and the people they met during that time often lead to them breaking up with their left-behind partners when home for the holiday, and then dating someone else on campus immediately after return on campus. A coincidence, I guess?

Tips for a Left-Behind Partner

So your boy- or girlfriend got into HBS and moves to Boston for school. You stay in the equivalent of Springfield and hope that the long-distance relationship will hold firm. Well, think again. Being a distant partner of a HBS student requires a lot of work – if you want things to work out that is. I have seen the relationships that made it through two years of HBS and I have seen those that didn't quite make it. The successful ones were those where the partner played it smart strategically. He/she would spend most weekends traveling to Boston in the early MBA days to get to know his partner's section-mates. He/she would try to become a familiar face around the partner, and he/she would become friends with the sharks around his/her partner, taking away a lot of the danger of his/her partner going wrong with one of them. It's all about determining your space – an important thing to do in the HBS dating scene.

Expanding the Fishing Pool

With only 40% of the student body at HBS being women, there is a disconnect between the number of males and females. Hence, for males, it is important to expand the fishing pool, which in the Cambridge area, with all the different schools, is not much of a challenge. Cambridge is full of interesting people, men and women, who are smart and occasionally good looking. Go fish!

93

The story of a cute international woman at HBS

Thanks to one of my HBS friends who helped me write this!

When I first asked this cute HBS woman (and now friend) for an interview on her HBS dating experiences, she responded that she didn't think her stories would be interesting enough, as she claimed to only have 'limited dating experience' at HBS. When I asked her what she called 'limited', her response was as follows:

- One relationship
- One real date
- One heart that I broke
- One broken heart myself
- Three friends with benefits (which she later had to correct to four)

When she confirmed with me that all these experiences involved HBS guys, I was sold! I told her she had an invaluable HBS dating/love life/benefits experience – or at least invaluable for the exercise I was working on. Here is her anonymous view on two years of closely interacting with HBS men.

To be able to capture her experiences not only in a qualitative but also in a quantitative way, I decided to expose her to the Lulu[166] test. Lulu allows women to rate men on a couple of dimensions – and so I asked her to rate her HBS men on some of these dimensions. Find an overview in the following graph:

---

166 Lulu is an online app that allows women to rate men they dated or went on a date with – consider it the Yelp for dating life.

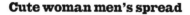

Cute woman men's spread

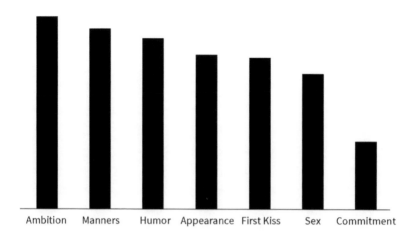

| Ambition | Manners | Humor | Appearance | First Kiss | Sex | Commitment |

**The aggregate score of all the men dated at HBS reveals some
outliers... The points were attributed by summing the score given to
the men on the different items listed, ranging from 1 to 10 (1 is very
low, 10 is very high) – thus the higher the score, the better.**

It is interesting how a couple of parameters stand out. On the positive
side, the HBS men she interacted with were ambitious and well-mannered.
And most of them seemed to be doing ok with making her laugh from time
to time – or maybe those were just the type of guys she was looking for. On
the downside, their sexual performances were not the best (for the record
– I was obviously not part of the group of men she is reporting on). The
main downer however is commitment (I already pointed out that issue in
a different context earlier). But be aware – this one data point is in no way
representative of the whole HBS crowd. I am sure that on average, the HBS
men are more than just ambitious and humorous!

94

The story of a good-looking international guy at HBS

Thanks to one of my HBS friends for writing this! Here are his uncensored thoughts on the HBS dating life.

"Coming from a rather conservative culture, single life at a school like HBS can be a bit overwhelming. While I didn't go to high school in the U.S., I did have some understanding of what to expect through my 'extensive research' from trashy Hollywood movies on the subject. Hence, I believe I could summarize dating life at HBS to be similar to dating at high school in the U.S. but WITH MONEY, NO PARENTS around and MUCH LESS RULES.

As a strategy consultant, I was looking for ways to summarize dating life at HBS through some kind of framework, and I found I could categorize people's dating mindset at HBS into four different groups:

1) **The I-am-here-to-play-group.** This group tends to be led by Europeans and (Latin-)Americans. They tend to focus on new experiences and the multi-cultural, inter-class exploration of the human anatomy. All styles are welcome, and this group even tends to develop some internal competition driven by unclear goals and parameters.

2) **The I-am-intrigued-to-know-what-is-out-there-group.** This group is not focused on sleeping around as much as the previous group, but is rather on the lookout for a long-term partner. They go out a lot, in the hope of meeting as many interesting people as possible, and who knows… the sought-after prince or princess might cross their path!

3) **The happy-couples-group.** They seem to have found their perfect other half – no playing, exploring or fooling around for them. Some of the other groups kind of envy them, as they seem to have found all the excitement of the HBS life without much of the drama and the searching. But I guess they face problems and frustrations of their own…

4) **The am-I-with-the-right-person-group?!?** People in this group have a partner but tend to behave as if they are part of group 1 or 2. People in this group usually tend to get into trouble without necessarily ac-

tively looking for it. HBS, full of smart people of which most try to be in shape, provides an environment where the sexual vibes tend to be on the high side.

Besides having different groups, there are also different timelines to look at:

1) **First few weeks at school.** The first weeks of school are completely crazy. Few people know each other, so they all interact with each other with little or no prejudice. No reputations have been created yet and hence the young well-groomed crowd of HBS students intermingle in the most interesting of ways during which many personal social interaction rules are broken. But for some reason all this seems to work – and it seems to make a lot of people happy. This is the prime time of dating life at HBS!

2) **The post-first-few-weeks-hangover.** Here comes the drama. At the end of September, sections have their section retreat, and it will change the dating scene dramatically. This is the point in time when the first section couples come out into the open. But more importantly, it is also the time when the section really forms. After this point, mingling outside one's own section becomes much harder as events start to become more section exclusive. Dating life, which had just peaked earlier, falls into a deep depression.

3) **Black Monday.** The Monday after Thanksgiving is when many people have found out that long distance dating is not working for them. Interestingly so, this pushes a lot of the people in earlier described groups 3 and 4 back into the first group, which creates a whole new set of dynamics and opportunities!

4) **Off-campus opportunities.** With things having found their way by year-end, it is the change of environment that pushes up a new wave of dating dynamics. Be it on a HBS-organized trip to the Bahamas or be it on the FIELD2 trip, these travels allow for easy cross-section interactions which again can bring fun and tears.

5) **Compressed carbon and kids.** The second semester of RC year sees a different kind of dynamic. Many of the people that came into school in a relationship see this as the perfect time of the year to get engaged (which

would allow them to get married right after school – perfect timing, no?). During this time, ever larger pieces of compressed carbon make their way to the fingers of someone in the section – and with it come all the discussions about wedding venues, dresses and cake frostings. It is also the time of the year where the first MBA offspring start making their appearance on school, which is actually very cool.

6) **And then there's the start of EC year.** Timing is crucial, as a new flock of RCs have just arrived on campus ready to be conquered and you don't want to be left with seconds. But it is also the time where people aggressively start looking for dating opportunities outside of HBS (think the Law School, Design School, Kennedy School and MIT).

7) **The rest of the year** is mostly about consolidating your gains or hunting for the ever rarer opportunities (mostly coming from cross-section travels).

So how would one best summarize two years of romantic life at HBS? Well, based on my fully unscientific approach of making an educated guess, I believe that on average the single and available person at HBS slept with about 3.5 HBS classmates over the two-year period. Many of them actually do get more than just sex and end up being engaged during or right after school (which for me also means I'll get another wedding invite in some part of the world soon). But overall I would say that my dating life at HBS was a very positive experience. Drama, tears and the risk of a minor STD are part of the game. And while it's not something HBS is meant to educate on, it is something that just happens when you have about 1,800 young talented people together in a small space and with free time on their hands. And to be honest, part of me misses those days..."

95

And then there are those that arrived having a partner already...

An important part of the student body arrives at HBS in one of the many non-single states. Some have their partner living with them in Boston, others have a somewhat distant or even overseas partner. There are those who are engaged or married. Some even have kids. Whatever non-single status they are in, they are not supposed to be part of the dating scene at HBS. I was one of those – and so I stayed away from the dating scene indeed! Nevertheless, I also have a story to tell – the story of the HBS student with a partner.

A first challenge is having your partner settle into the new environment. In my case, that was not too much of a problem. My partner was American, was accepted to a Master's program at nearby MIT, and had lived in Cambridge before. For others, life as a partner of a HBS student can be tough. There are students' wives who gave up their careers to move to Boston with their husband (and kids). There is the Japanese wife who moved to Cambridge but couldn't speak a word of English and had a hard time settling in. There is the guy who moved to Boston with his wife from Poland, and while he did have a permit to stay in the U.S., he was not allowed to work on U.S. soil (with the exception of some jobs linked to HBS). There is this other partner who decided to stay in China instead of following his wife to the U.S., after 4 years of marriage – they met up once during the two year MBA program – their marriage survived! Partners of HBS students often have a more difficult time adjusting to the new setting created by HBS than the HBS students themselves, as they don't necessarily have the same social network and career opportunities their beloved ones do.

Because of that, HBS makes genuine efforts to accommodate partners as much as possible, and then definitely those living with the students on or around campus. First, there are some of the practical benefits, such as the possibility to sign your partner up on the HBS healthcare plan available to students. What I was really impressed with – based on the feedback I got from my partner was the pro-activeness of the Partner Club at HBS. This club provides information and activities for the partners to help them integrate into the new environment. And indeed, in the period leading up to the start of school, my partner seemed to have as many invites to social activities from the Partner Club as I got from the Student Association! I don't know if it's thanks to the Partner Club at HBS, but most of the couples that moved to Cambridge together, did survive the MBA experience.

There are different ways students manage the presence of their partner at HBS. Some students take their partners along to almost every single event – it almost felt as if they were part of our section or our HBS class for that matter. For others, I barely knew they had a partner (or came to believe they had made their partner up) as I never saw them. As far as I am concerned, I brought my partner to the bigger events, but she wasn't too keen on coming along to all of the section events, though she didn't like me coming home late and drunk from them either.

Managing a relationship at HBS is an art – nevertheless this period in life can also be the best time to really enjoy each other's presence. Never again might you have as much liberty and free time to do things together as a couple. No wonder so many people eventually get engaged!

96

Sexual harassment at HBS

Dating and flirting is fun and harmless most of the time. Unfortunately, there are also cases where things get out of control. In an environment like HBS, where you have a concentration of strong personalities from all continents, some activities that started out with innocent intentions can sometimes end up as cases of sexual harassment. It is an important issue, and one that the HBS administration takes seriously.

I personally didn't observe any instance of sexual harassment at HBS – though I did hear the stories. I cannot comment more on what did or did not happen. What I do know, is that HBS has different campaigns going on on-campus to discuss the issue – the most memorable one was the "TELL SOMEONE" campaign. This campaign focused on students coming forward with their stories to the HBS administration. With students coming from very different parts of the world, having them come forward is not always an obvious thing because of cultural and/or religious reasons.

Another communication channel on the topic was through email – Youngme Moon, a star professor at HBS and one of the leaders within the HBS administration, wrote a letter to the MBA crowd in which she made some strong statements:

"Sexual assault happens at HBS. Every year. Without exception."

In the letter, she gives examples of what sexual harassment is – the definition is much broader than rape or unwanted physical contact. She talks about the impact it can have on victims and their lives. She also mentions resources which are available for victims, while also pointing out the disciplinary actions in place for those that take on the role of aggressor. Finally, she discusses the launch of the "Be safe. Be sure." campaign on campus – a campaign that was the result of several discussions held between the student body and the HBS administration.

As described in the previous chapters, dating life at HBS can be exciting. Let's keep it that way.

PART

XII

HBS GRADES – DO
THEY MATTER?

97

HBS: standing out before and during the MBA

Some of you are probably applying to HBS at this time. It's a wrestle against standardized exams such as the TOEFL and GMAT, nights spent on essay (re-)writing and tons of mock interviews before clearing the last interview hurdle. All these efforts serve only one goal – to stand out amongst the thousands of applicants. Those of you who manage to make it beyond the admissions cliffs will be part of the next HBS class. Congratulations.

And then one day, you find yourself amongst the 'survivors' of this competitive selection process and part of the HBS student body. And again, it's about standing out. You can do so by being the master of parties, or being Vice-President of one of the clubs. A more academic approach of standing out however would be through grades and honors. Here's how this works at HBS. For each course, students at HBS fall in one of the following four categories:

- Category I — given to the top 15-20% of students
- Category II — given to the next 70-75% of students
- Category III — given to the lowest-performing 10% of students
- Category IV — seldom assigned; designates failure

While grading can vary among courses, class participation typically accounts for 40 to 60 percent of a course grade while the balance comes from exams or exercises.

Class participation is probably the trickiest one to nail. It is about finding the right balance between quantity and quality of comments. Getting to speak in class and thus boosting your class grade requires a strategy. As classes are moderated by professors, it is about finding the right technique to get the professor's attention and to raise your hand at the best possible moment. Don't overdo it (having your hand up all the time will not help you getting called on). Others try to get called on with exaggerated gestures or by continuously staring at the professor. From my experience, it is more about raising your hand when things get more technical/difficult and thus there are less 'hands in the air'. As such, my advice would be not to waste your call on the straightforward comments. Focus on value add! While class performance is a daily headache, every couple of months there is also a series of exams to deal with.

When discussing HBS grades, it is also important to discuss if and why they matter. 95% of the HBS class will graduate at the end of the 2-year MBA. Some will do so with honors – a small percentage will do with HBS's top academic honor – the Baker Scholar (top 5% of the class). Is the extra effort worth it to be part of that top 5%? Or does one just need to stay away out of the bottom 5%?

From my experience, I did not have any company or employer ask me about my HBS grades. Similarly, I haven't heard any of my fellow students mention it. Moreover, as most students get a job before graduation, they wouldn't even be able to disclose their scores to their potential future employer. Grades at HBS are more about personal honor, or only relevant for those wanting to pursue an academic career. Finally, for those in it for the money, I haven't seen any research that demonstrates correlation between being a Baker Scholar and increased earnings for that matter[167]! So why put so much effort in getting great HBS grades!?!

Overall I am very positive about the HBS grading system. As described above, 90% of students will have a grade in either category I or II, removing a lot of the stress related to exams, yet creating the required incentive for students to prepare for classes and exams. Compared to my European college experience, where up to 50% of students would fail certain classes, the HBS grading method allows for more focus on learning rather than proficiency in taking exams. As a student, I am very happy that the focus of my academic HBS experience is on the former and that I'm not spending $200,000 to learn how to ace exams.

---

167 As far as I know...

98

HBS exams and how to best prepare for them

In the interactive case-based educational system at HBS, exams seem to be a bit of an outlier. Yet they do exist, and preparing for them at HBS is not as straightforward as in an educational system that relies solely on books and class notes. Some professors do send us class summaries, or an overview of key formulas to use for a finance class. But the real magic comes from alternative resources – student groups that pull together useful summary notes on a class and share them accordingly.

I found the best class notes to be the ones distributed by the WSA – the Women Students Association at HBS. They have been very active in creating useful class notes, and they made them available free of charge to everyone – yes, even males! Interestingly, they would put some kind of commercials in it. For instance, the first slide of the PowerPoint slide deck would contain a commercial for their upcoming conference – clever marketing ladies! Besides the ones I got from the WSA, I also relied on other sources of exam notes, such as my discussion group members or section-mates.

As grades don't matter all that much at HBS – or at least not as much compared to college for example – students tend to openly share notes and advice for exams. Another contributing factor to this is the fact that the exams themselves at HBS are case-based – hence the preparation part for an exam can be considered less important than with traditional exams based on formulas and exercises.

I prepared for my exams in the most 'stressless' way. I would go through summary notes I got from one of my sources, read up on some of my own scribbles taken during class and have a look at the summaries sent from professors. For the more technical classes, such as our finance and operations class, where mathematical formulas come into play, I would prepare a 1-page summary with the formulas that were most commonly used in class. Most professors allow the use of a formula sheet at the exam.

On a final note, the setting of HBS exams differ a lot from my experience with college exams in Europe. Exams are held in a classroom without the presence of professors or assistants, leaving a lot of room for potential cheating. On top of that, a lot of the exams can be taken from home at HBS (or from wherever the students find convenient). Students can download the exam from a given time and upload their responses as a PDF document before the defined end time of the exam. HBS seems to trust students to respect the HBS values of honesty and mutual respect. In contrast, my experience from taking exams in my former college in Europe was very different. Students were spread out over a room to prevent the possibility of cheating. And of course students would not be left alone in a room without any 'academic surveillance'.

Overall, my exams at HBS were the least stressful of my whole life-long academic career. Not only because they only accounted for a certain percentage of the grade (next to the class contribution), but also because of the fact that the outcome of the exams wouldn't play a major role in my future. Hence, my final advice for the HBS exams would be – relax, read through some notes, and have a piece of chocolate!

The first Harvard midterms – do I really belong here?

My very first exam was not the typical exam you would expect at HBS – it was not case-based! Indeed, as a kind of mid-term check in the first year at HBS, HBS organizes an exam for the operations class that is a traditional multiple choice exam. It involves traditional questions, some math and very traditional options between answers a/b/c/d.

A couple of days later, I received my score: 19/20! Waaaoooow!!! I scored 19/20 on an exam at HBS! I must be some kind of genius. At least, that's what I thought until I saw the average score on the exam: 19/20 as well! Wow… never ever had I completed an exam on which the average was that high. Was the exam too easy? Or is the HBS crowd just so intelligent that they perform great on all exams? I think the former is closer to the truth.

I wonder about the point of an exam where everybody has an almost perfect score. I came from an educational culture where a 14/20 is a very good performance. 16/20 is brilliant. 18/20 is top-class performance and is only achieved by the 1 or 2 top students. What is the point of having an exam where there is no differentiation between students? Is it considered a learning exercise? Is it to make everybody feel good? Where is the sense of competition in a school that is extremely competitive just to get in?

I believe HBS does not want to use exams as a differentiator, rather as a tool to make sure students review some of their notes so they can participate in class. As far as I am concerned, I am fine with that. It sure as hell takes away a lot of the stress. I just wish I hadn't looked at the average score. I still would have thought of myself as a genius...

100

Creative ways of grading – beyond class participation

I like the concept of class participation being a key measure for grades, and resent the old-fashioned approach of written exams. But there are even better ways of grading than class participation alone. I am a fan of business schools rating their students on the creation of business value in the real world. Or have them sell/import/produce something. Or have them trade stocks and reward them on the results. Turns out that HBS already applies a lot of these grading techniques in its MBA program. And I love it!

A class on quantifying the valuation of companies for example requires students to choose a stock to buy or sell and to document their findings. On the last day of class, students have to pitch their stock to peers, with these other students rating the content and the presentation of the pitch. A course on investment strategies challenges students to get the best return in a simulated financial environment. A negotiations class has students compete for a free dinner with the professor based on performance in the weekly negotiations sessions with other students. The FIELD program at

HBS, with students working on consultancy projects for external companies in emerging markets, has these companies grade the students on their final recommendations. I found these alternative ways of grading much more motivating than the standard written exam. And they also reflect how students are likely to be 'graded' in their future professional lives.

101

The honors for the not-so-honor-able...

While I didn't care much about grading or honors during my time at HBS, there was one moment when I actually regretted not having done better at my exams – graduation. It was not so much because of what was written on my diploma – rather it had to do with the public way in which the honors were being called out. Here's kind of how things went for me – how about this for an awkward moment!?!

Below is an extract from the graduation ceremony, as announced by the speaker[168]:

Vanessa Lack	highest honors
Colin Lorie	honors
Carla Maas	highest honors
Frederic Mahieu	**(silence)**
John Nittman	honors

Let's just say I was unlucky enough to have my last name preceded and followed by people that had done really well at HBS. Damn you alphabet!

---

168 All names are made up and thus fully fictional – except for mine!

XIII

HBS'S NATURAL ENVIRONMENT – CAMBRIDGE AND SURROUNDINGS

102

More than just a place to study – also a place to live!

Cambridge hosts some of the most prestigious schools of the world, including Harvard and MIT. For the tens of thousands of students these schools attract, Cambridge is more than a place to study – it is also a place where they will live for a couple of years.

For HBS students, there are different housing options to consider. The first option is the HBS dorms. The dorms are located on-campus and each student is given a small room with a 1-person bed, a wardrobe, a shower and a desk to work on. However, the dorms have big and comfy common rooms that have spacious and well-equipped kitchens, couches and tables – most of them even have a piano! The dorms are a great option for the younger students who don't mind sharing facilities with others. It is also by far the most affordable option, with the additional advantage that students can take a 10-month lease instead of a standard 12-month one.[169] According to HBS, 80% of students live in some kind of on-campus housing.

Another HBS housing option is the HBS apartments. These can be found both on and off-campus. The on-campus apartments are mostly in the Soldiers Field Park buildings or in the more modern One Western Ave building – not sure why HBS couldn't come up with cooler sounding names for those. The buildings themselves have well-equipped apartments and come in different sizes and layouts – 1, 2 or 3-bedroom apartments. They are relatively pricey (but still below market rates for the area) and small. On the other hand, they are conveniently located on-campus. The off-campus accommodations are mostly smaller buildings or houses that are located within walking distance of campus. Rent has to be paid for the full 12 months, even if students are not around for the summer months.

Finally, there is the private market. Students opt for private rentals for different reasons. First, they want something a bit fancier[170]. Second, they

---

169   Find out more about housing here: **http://goo.gl/O5XWYO**
170   One of my section-mates even lived in the Ritz-Carlton in Boston.

want to live in a different part of town or just away from campus. Third, they got a bad pick at the HBS housing priority choosing lottery, leaving them with old and overpriced options on the HBS list to choose from.

I did not live on campus, nor did I live in HBS housing (mostly for the third reason). And looking back at it, I was happy not to. I lived at Central Square, a 15 to 20 minute walk from the HBS campus, but conveniently located a 10 minute walk from Harvard Square, close to public transportation, shops and nice restaurants.

Most of all, I was happy to escape from the HBS bubble when going home at night. As one of the older students, I did not feel the need to have a 100% HBS life – rather, I loved spending a big part of my life on campus, while having my home in the 'real world'. As such, I managed to keep in touch with reality outside of the HBS bubble, which was important to me. And I would see the campus on a daily basis anyway, going there on my daily walk dressed in layers of clothes and snow boots…

However, for the average international student, finding private housing is not all that simple. I was lucky to have an American girlfriend who was able to fly to Boston for an apartment hunt prior to the start of school. She also helped with the ease of completing the paperwork (Cambridge landlords know that demand for housing exceeds supply in Cambridge, so some of them avoid having to deal with foreigners if possible) and taught me how to write a check to pay rent[171].

One final hint: with temperatures going well below the freezing point for the majority of the year, make sure the place you rent has a good heating system and has basic insulation – trust me, I had my share of heating problems to deal with. With Cambridge houses often being very old, some of them tend to lose heat faster than the heater can produce. Make sure to keep warm!

---

171 Yes, I had to pay rent by writing a check on a monthly basis. Never before in my life had I written a check. This practice is uncommon in most parts of Europe (and the rest of the world for as far as I know) – we all prefer wire transfers. However, the U.S. (one of the most developed places on earth) still seems very fond of using checks…

103

Getting around the HBS campus

Ah, the Harvard Business School campus. I remember vividly how I had no idea what to expect of the campus on my first visit to the school. I was only going to campus that day to visit the school and to sit in on one of the classes; I was far from being part of the HBS crowd at that time. Sure, I had seen images of the iconic Baker library building, but that was all I could imagine at that point.

For some reason, I thought gaining access to the campus would be a difficult endeavor. A place as famous as Harvard Business School must have some access control to its campus, right? Turns out, most of the buildings open to students are also open to the wider public – i.e. all doors open without the need for credentials or a cardkey of sorts[172].

Google maps offers a good depiction of the site – the best way to virtually look at the site however is on the HBS website, where a map of the campus can be found[173]. What can't be seen on the map though, is the whole grid of underground tunnels that exist between buildings. With temperatures going as low as -20 degrees Celsius / -4 degrees Fahrenheit in winter and snow piling up in the streets, these tunnels are a real treat, especially for those living on campus. I will never forget how easy it was to differentiate those living on and off campus. The classroom would have some people arriving for class wearing snow boots and several layers of clothing. Others would walk in with nothing more than shorts, a T-shirt and flip-flops – they could use the tunnel system to reach class without having to set foot outside!

---

172   This is the case during the day on weekdays only.
173   Find the map here: **http://goo.gl/8VKAVV**

104

The HBS campus surroundings

Besides the campus itself, it is interesting to note that the HBS campus is somewhat isolated from other parts of Harvard. Indeed, HBS is on the other side of the River Charles. It's about a 10-minute walk away from Harvard Square and Harvard Yard, the real 'Harvard Downtown Area'. This is where you see most of the Harvard students studying in Starbucks or other cafes. This is where a lot of the dinner and dance parties happen. And this is where you get a real city feel, contrary to the calm and quiet of the HBS campus.

But most of all, Harvard Square is a nice place for a stroll while enjoying the views and the unique energy of the area. Come and visit Harvard Square, just like thousands of tourists do each year. From early May till late September, Harvard is flooded with people who are interested to see what Cambridge is all about. And it seems that a vast majority of them come from as far as Asia – armed with guides and cameras!

105

The Coop – a Harvard/MIT landmark

The Coop is a cooperative that manages a couple of stores in and around Harvard and MIT. They mostly sell books and all kinds of Harvard or MIT branded products. Most of all, the Coop has become a landmark in Harvard Square and a must-go for the occasional visitor in Cambridge. The stylish building it is located in attracts people from everywhere. Interestingly so, the Coop was founded in the late 19th century by students for students. Still today, The Coop's mission is to serve the Harvard and MIT communities as a cooperative, by providing quality products and services. Meanwhile, it has grown into one of America's largest chain of campus stores. It is an ideal place to buy some of the typical junk one doesn't actually need (do you really need Harvard branded golf balls?) – but who cares about that anyway!?! My personal favorite? The HAHVAHD shirts – as a non-native English speaker, I indeed cannot pronounce those English R's in the correct manner…

106

Students' favorite hangouts

Most of the favorite HBS student hangouts are located in and around the Harvard Square area. I loved that area – there must not be many other places in the world that have such a high concentration of energy and brain power.

Of course, most of these venues offer drinks. The best place for a late-night drink/dance/hookup is the Kong. Located close to Harvard Square above an Asian restaurant, the Kong (full name – Hong Kong) is a multi-floor dance bar famous for its good dance music and its scorpion bowl – a famous drink which I remember more for its alcohol content than taste.

There are a lot of other unique places around the Square. Typically, most sections end up having one or two fixed places where they congregate. Our section was an avid fan of the Boat House, close to the Square as well.

During the day, I mostly spent time reading cases in one of the three (!) local Starbucks. The biggest one is located in the middle of Harvard Square, offering a view from the second floor that can't be beaten!

107

There are brains on the other side of the river – MIT

There is this other school in Cambridge that has quite the international reputation as well. MIT, short for Massachusetts Institute of Technology, is everything that Harvard is not and vice versa. Harvard is the school of the well-spoken ones. MIT has the reputation to be the school of the nerds and the engineers. I guess the truth is somewhere in between, but

MIT is part of the HBS experience, if only because MIT students are great to have a laugh with[174]...

First of all, there's the MIT campus itself, with its iconic dome and its even more iconic nerdy types hanging around it. Life at MIT is hard – so hard that students barely have time to rest. And if they find a minute to take a nap, somebody has started capturing those moments. Find an ode to sleeping MIT beauties here: **http://goo.gl/ulfROi**

Second, there's the dress code. One can almost tell if someone is from MIT by the way they are dressed. The fancy shoes or clothes of Harvard make way for the comfy sweater and sweatpants of MIT. The organizers of the MIT gala event even had to explicitly state that students had to dress classy for that event on the invite!

Finally, MIT is all about engineering, and one running joke about that is the new measure of length developed by MIT students in the fifties: the Smoot. I first discovered the Smoots when walking over the Charles Bridge, connecting Cambridge with downtown Boston across the River Charles. It started as a fraternity prank where students laid down student Oliver Smoot on the bridge repeatedly, to measure the length of the bridge by using his height. They then named this new measurement after Oliver Smoot, then 5 feet 7 inches tall (1m70). The bridge was exactly 364.4 Smoots long plus one ear. The fraternity painted the Smoot marks on the bridge with intervals of 10 Smoots. For decades now, these have been repainted by the student body of MIT. The Smoot has become a Boston legend. And interestingly so, Oliver Smoot ended up becoming the chairman of the American National Standards Institute and president of the International Organization for Standardization![175]

---

174 This works both ways. There are T-shirts for sale at the MIT bookstore that read: "Harvard: because not everyone can get into MIT"

175 Find out more on the Smoots here:

http://goo.gl/BMZvof   **http://goo.gl/b3pU8x**   **http://goo.gl/L7Wgpa**

108

Getting around Cambridge

With the HBS campus somewhat out of the way of where the real action is (think restaurants, places to have drinks, etc.), it is important to find convenient modes of transportation around Cambridge and Boston. And we will be focusing here on the more ecologic and economic (parking in Boston/Cambridge costs a fortune) ways of getting around:

Self-powered tools

A bike remains a great means of transportation. Personally, I did not own a bike in Cambridge, but I did make use of Hubway, a bike-sharing service with docking stations all over town. It is affordable and convenient – though a lot of the docking stations close during winter. The whole system shuts down when expecting adverse weather – making it an unreliable transportation option at times.[176]

The ultimate way of self-powered propulsion is to walk! I have never walked as much in my life as I did in my two years in Cambridge. I often preferred walking compared to the bikes because of the weather – riding a bike in freezing temperatures is not only a safety hazard, but also a freezing-to-death hazard!

Sharing tools

The new economy is all about sharing. Students share cabs, but they also use apps to book transportation through services like Uber and Lyft, where a driver would pick you up and bring you to your destination using his personal car. Another way of sharing, if you prefer driving yourself, is to rent a car. The most convenient service here is Zipcar, a service that has different cars parked all over town in strategic spots where students can rent a car on an hourly basis. It is an ideal means of transportation for shopping in

---

176 In recent years though, Hubway has tried to keep more and more stations open during the winter months.

bulk or a quick drive around town. However, the administrative workload for international students to sign up for this service can be a hassle.

Public tools

Boston is home to the oldest subway system in the U.S. Close to the HBS campus is the Harvard Square stop, on the Red Line of the MBTA (known locally as the T)[177], connecting Harvard and Cambridge to downtown Boston. Alternatively, bus line 1 takes students to downtown Boston as well.

Harvard tools

Harvard itself manages a sizeable transportation network of its own. It operates a dozen shuttle buses driving across town connecting its different campuses in Cambridge and its surroundings. One of these shuttles passes through the HBS campus. The shuttles can be very convenient at times. Their routes as well as the actual location of the buses can easily be tracked on the Harvard app.

109

Event-mania – Cambridge as a great (non-alcoholic) host

Cambridge hosts two of the most reputable educational institutions of the world – Harvard and MIT. Hence, there is an important need for adequate venues to organize conferences, receptions and drinks. As most student clubs organize events on tight budgets, the schools themselves provide locations to organize events – and some of these happen to be really nice! My personal favorite is the Harvard Centre of European Studies. Conveniently located close to Harvard Yard, the center offers a really nice building with a very spacious and functional layout for organizing events. What really stands out is their garden. The garden is maintained to perfection, decorat-

---

177 MBTA is the Massachusetts Bay Transportation Authority and is the operator of public transportation in Boston and surroundings.

ed with statues and a fountain, which makes it a great place for a speaker event in early autumn or late spring.

Other locations that stand out are the central aula of the Harvard Kennedy School, the Harvard Faculty Club and the MIT Media Lab. Last but not least, some of the common spaces in the residential buildings on the HBS campus provide an ideal location for organizing events as well.

While free, there is a downside to using these locations compared to off campus spaces. None of them allow the consumption of alcohol (except when hiring a person licensed to do so – which can easily add a couple of hundreds of dollars to the bill). As a European, I always struggled to understand the tight alcohol laws in the U.S. – but then again, I just had to adapt. On the positive side, all of those places are surrounded by bars and pubs with plenty of alcohol to continue celebrating the event afterwards anyway... as long as you are 21, that is[178]!

HBS carefully controls its on-site alcohol prohibition. An infamous event happened after the HBS Show a couple of years ago. The cleaning staff found several empty alcohol containers in Burden Auditorium after the show. No one had reported drunk students that night within HBS premises, nor was there any damage or any reports related to improper behavior. However, the presidents of the HBS show (HBS students who voluntarily take on that leadership role) were told that their inability to prevent alcohol consumption that night on HBS premises represented "failed leadership" and an "inability to uphold HBS Community Values". They were banned from attending all non-academic social activities and placed on probation until graduation[179].

HBS's stand in this case opens an interesting debate on leadership. Are leaders responsible for the acts of the people they lead? Should CEOs resign when fraudulent actions occur within their organizations, despite not being directly aware of them? HBS's response to these questions, judging from the above case at the HBS show, seems clear: YES! Leadership is more than providing the troops with clear guidance and goals. Leadership is also about creating a culture upholding strong values, or having a system in

---

178 It is illegal to drink alcohol in the U.S. for anyone younger than 21.
179 Find a Harbus article on the matter here: **http://goo.gl/WvF1MB**

place that provides the necessary controls for prevention or early detection of bad behaviors. And to a certain extent I do agree with that. Though I wonder – in this day and age where a lot of academic research is under scrutiny for data integrity, would Dean Nohria have to resign if one of his professors cheated in a publication? And would that be the right thing to do? Let's have some further thoughts about this over a glass of beer...[180]

110

Technology is the new... natural environment at HBS?

One of my EC courses at HBS was called Competing with Social Networks. I took this course because I frankly don't know all that much about social media. I check my Facebook account once a month, I have an occasional look on Yelp before booking a table in a restaurant and while I have heard about the newer tools such as Instagram and Vine, I have never used them. I realized that my limited use of social media was not quite the norm at HBS. But with businesses from all over the world making tons of money through the use of social media, I figured it wouldn't hurt to improve my understanding of what social media is really all about; hence my decision to enroll in this class. And I have to admit, the class left me with some interesting insights – did you know for example that much of Facebook's initial success is linked to the feature enabling people to secretively stalk one another? Crazy no?

This course not only broadened my knowledge on social media and social strategies through case studies – it also forced me to use social media myself. To complete the course, I had to become an expert in some of the social media tools. I could choose from different options, such as becoming an elite contributor on Yelp, to become famous on YouTube and sell over $500 of merchandise that way, or even practicing to become a social game specialist. I chose the first option and worked hard to try and get my Yelp elite status! On a personal level, the class inspired me to further experi-

---

180 If you are over 21 that is...

ment with some social media tools, and I hence created a Twitter account that I linked to my blog hbstimes.com. Quite the adventure for a social media dinosaur like me!

Overall, the use of social media is widespread at HBS. The vast majority of students are on Facebook – for socializing but also for planning and communicating events, section activities AND even to share class content and discussions. Then there is the use of Tumblr for more entertaining snapshots of life at HBS (find the WhatShouldWeCallHBS Tumblr link here: **http://goo.gl/mrdXTw** with some of my favorite posts here: **http://goo.gl/ZEYppl** and here: **http://goo.gl/AlDNEz**). Other popular social media are GroupMe, WhatsApp, Instagram and LinkedIn. And with the HBS campus being located far away from the places to go in Boston, taxi-apps such as Uber and Lyft are on a roll as well. YouTube is the favorite destination for those fun 'last-class-of-the-semester' videos. Finally, sex always sells, even at HBS – find the Fifty Shades of Finance written by HBS students here: **http://goo.gl/GnwPui**

Technology is not only the new environment at HBS; it is also the new way of dating! Tinder, Grinder, OkCupid, specific websites and apps that provide a dating service for people in Ivy League schools only (which they verify through your email address), etc. Dating happens more and more online. Interestingly so, some people are using their association with Harvard on these online platforms – it seems like a great way to attract the opposite sex! Though I have heard some complaints on the role of technology in the dating scene: one girl couldn't get over the fact that she got invited on a date by means of a Microsoft Outlook calendar invite! Has technology become too much of a natural environment to HBS students? Where is the romance in this, guys?

111

Boston – home to big brains and strong muscles!

The Boston warea not only houses some of the best schools in the U.S., it is also home to some of the best sports team of popular American sports.

There is the Boston Red Sox, a legendary baseball team playing its home games at Fenway Park close to downtown Boston. I was not familiar with the sport before moving to the U.S., and was surprised to learn that the average baseball-game can last for hours and hours (and people just move around the stadium during the game, occasionally heading out for a drink or some food). While I don't think baseball will ever be my favorite sport, I did enjoy the atmosphere at Fenway Park and would recommend all HBS students to enjoy an afternoon of baseball while in Boston. And if the Red Sox make it to the final of the World Series (as they did during my time in Boston), definitely head out to a sports bar to experience the game with the local fans! Go Red Sox!

Northeast from Fenway park is the TD Garden – home of the Boston Celtics. The Celtics are the most successful team in the history of the NBA and still today have one of the better basketball sides in the field. I enjoyed the sport, the atmosphere and the entertainment during the many breaks.

For the ice hockey fans, Boston has the Boston Bruins to offer. With the Bruins winning a Division and a Conference Championship during my time there, there was much to celebrate! Finally, the New England Patriots contribute to Boston's sports legacy in football, being one of the most successful football teams in the U.S. history with no less than four Super Bowl victories! To date, I am still wondering how Boston ended up having this many successful sports teams. Maybe a good idea to write a business case about this, HBS?

PART

XIV

AND NOW, THE
END IS NEAR...

112

The final class of the year – an emotional moment for students...

The last class of each course at HBS is always a bit emotional. Typically, this last class will start with a final summary of the course, followed by a goodbye speech and/or advice from the professor. Twenty minutes before the end of class, professors will end their speech, take their stuff, say goodbye and walk out of the room. Students are left with a link to an online evaluation system where they can review both the professor and the course.

While the evaluation is standard, the professor's speech is not. Some have very inspiring messages they share with us. Others have a more rational approach to the final speech. Of the more than 20 HBS classes I had, I tried to write down some of the most inspiring pieces of advice given by some of the top business educators of the world. Find your free 'lecture' below:

- When showing the picture of an imperfectly made clay pot – "Live life with great purpose but imperfectiously"
- "Try to make problems as visible as possible"
- "Never compromise on fun, love, humor"
- "Take accountability for changing the system you are in"
- "Once you start lying, you are screwed"
- A quote from Oscar Wilde – "I can resist anything but temptation"
- On how to be successful in life – "You need an overall great theory and a little tiny bit of proof that it works in real life"

During RC year, the section atmosphere allows for some additional entertainment during last classes. Professors tend to be offered a gift, ranging from a bottle of wine (after having taught a case on a famous wine bottler) or a framed version of a case study signed by all students in class (a HBS tradition the first time a professor teaches his or her new case). Some professors even get dragged into watching a full-blown PowerPoint presentation on the topic of … them! But in the end, they all leave with a huge standing ovation.

The very last class during RC year (as well as a specifically arranged section class event at the end of EC year) ends with an extended version of a SkyDeck session. Professors, fellow students, HBS in general… all are featured and are mocked. A great way to end a semester, a school year…even a the full-blown HBS experience. Find some online examples on You- Tube here: **http://goo.gl/R3VqUv** (notice the big panda in b the room at one minute) and **http://goo.gl/aRdppe** (at 45 seconds)

113

The final class of the year – an emotional moment for professors...

The standard format of the last class of the year is sometimes interrupted by a personal announcement of a professor. During my two years at HBS, I can remember as many as three professors making a goodbye speech – they too had just spent some of their last moments in a HBS classroom. The type of the announcement differs between staff, as does the reason given for the departure. One professor said he got an offer he couldn't refuse from another business school. Another said it was time for her and her family to return to her roots and family in Europe. Finally, one professor was clear and honest about the reason for his departure – he was told he wouldn't make tenure.

Life for junior faculty at Harvard is hard. They have about eight years to become a tenured professor at the school – and as with most management consulting jobs, it is an 'up or out' system. Fail to reach your required number and quality of publications along the way and you can go. If you don't have what it takes to make the cut, you are pushed out. There are some running jokes about how hard it is to get tenure at Harvard. A junior Harvard professor that wants to get a mortgage gets reassured by the lender, saying that it is ok as he can get a variable rate (as he likely won't stay at Harvard for more than a couple of years)[181]. Another joke is that at most universities, you have to write a book to get tenure, while at Harvard, they have to write a book about you.[182]

Interestingly so, this status in academics was established in the late 1700s to protect academic freedom at religious schools[183]. However, its benefits, which include life-long employment, seem outstripped by some of the disadvantages such as decreased competition amongst academics, etc. Despite how hard it is to get tenure at Harvard, the Harvard brand name still manages to attract talented individuals from all over the world that want access to the Harvard community.

114

HBS commencement[184] – a jump into a new life... and into the River Charles

Graduating from Harvard Business School is all about putting on a graduation gown, listening to speeches and jumping into a new part of life... as well as jumping into the River Charles. It is a tradition for students gradu-

---

181　**http://goo.gl/J88vcH**
182　**http://goo.gl/j3lIVD**
183　**http://goo.gl/Dk9ERZ**
184　Commencement – another one of these weird words I had never heard before. According to dictionary.com commencement is 'an act or instance of commencing; beginning' as well as 'the ceremony of conferring degrees or granting diplomas at the end of the academic year'.

181

182

183

ating from the Harvard schools to jump into this river right next to the HBS campus. Only when I was standing on top of the footbridge over the River Charles in the middle of the night did I realize how high this bridge is, and how scary it is to take this big jump. But I did it. And there probably isn't a more symbolic jump to take than this one.[185]

Of course, the official commencement ceremonies at Harvard are anything but about taking a dive. Most of the celebrations were concentrated on May 29th. At 6.30AM, the graduating Business School students gathered on the HBS campus before they walked over to Harvard Yard. A couple of hours later, Harvard Yard was filled with thousands of students (as well as family and friends) from all Harvard schools. During the ceremony students received their graduation blessing from Harvard's president, Drew Gilpin Faust. She announced the official graduation of the students, school by school. The rest of the ceremony consisted primarily of speeches and giving honorary doctoral degrees to some of the distinguished guests – during my graduation, these guests included Aretha Franklin, Michael Bloomberg and George Bush senior (Aretha Franklin even sang the national anthem!).

Commencement speeches are a big thing in the U.S. and schools invite some top-notch speakers – ideally alums – to talk about their experiences and give a motivational speech. At Harvard, these speakers often include big names, think Bill Gates, J.K. Rowling, Alan Greenspan and Opraaaaaah Winfrey. And most of them cater to what they believe they have been hired for: giving a huge motivational boost to some of the brightest grads in the world. And if you don't know what I am talking about, just check out some Harvard commencement speeches on YouTube. Although the most famous graduation speech of them all took place at the other end of the U.S., when Steve Jobs delivered his speech at Stanford's graduation in 2005[186].

In Europe, we don't have this tradition of commencement speeches. Some schools might have a professor say a few words. But the graduation most often seems to be a low-budget / low-time-investment event. Gowns are not common at all in continental Europe, and while most students will

---

185 Please consider the dangers linked to this jump – this writing is in no means meant to incite people to do this.
186 **http://goo.gl/YfJ8xL**

make some effort to dress up for the ceremony, you will struggle to find students wearing full-blown suits with ties. Degrees are not handed over to students on the stage, but after the 10 minute ceremony in a small office, where they are all stacked in boxes[187]. Some schools are known to just send their degrees by mail.

At Harvard, the whole ceremony is just huge! All Harvard grads – be it from Harvard College, Law School, Medical School, etc. come together in Harvard Yard for the celebration. The school even publishes a special commencement edition newspaper for the event. And limos can be spotted all around Harvard yard bringing in distinguished guests. Police are omnipresent to organize the flow of thousands of students, family, friends and VIPs. There are huge flat-screen TVs so everyone can follow the event – even the ones with the crappy seats in the back. There is respect paid to all kinds of traditions (like a guy thumping a stick on the ground repeatedly to officially open the ceremony). And to keep things entertaining, there are students playing tricks on each other. One of my section-mates had his chair disappear after he – and the whole student body with him – had stood up for a round of applause. The foldable chair had been duly hidden under someone's gown for most of the ceremony (these things do have practical use after all!). Meanwhile, while searching for this chair, my unfortunate section-mate was hopping from one lap to the other. Oh, and there were flags! Did I mention the flags!?! All students had a little Harvard flag to wave in the air! They added to the whole experience and made me feel like I was at a soccer game back home. And who doesn't like the great atmosphere of a soccer game!?

After the Harvard commencement ceremony, the different schools return to their respective campuses for lunch and for the individual school commencement speeches, as well as for the official handover of the Harvard certificate. One by one, students lined up to go on stage. Someone states your name over the microphone[188], someone else hands you your degree, and Dean Nohria himself concludes the deal by giving a strong

---

187 This is what my graduation from a Belgian college looked like.
188 It is difficult to get all those names right with people from literally all over the world graduating from HBS. Rumor goes that HBS hires a linguist who practices the pronunciation of names for days prior to the ceremony.

handshake. There's only so much time left for a quick wave to the public and a quick smile to the camera.

And off you go. Things need to progress quickly. With 900 students receiving their degree, spending six seconds a student already stretches the ceremony to about 1.5 hours. Add that to some more speeches and things quickly become dull.

Personally, I enjoyed most of my commencement day. It was fun struggling to get into a gown for the first time. I enjoyed waving my little Harvard flag during the commencement ceremony. I was proud to get on stage to pick up my degree. But let's face it – deep down, I am still the shy, introverted, down-to-earth European to whom most of the motivational speeches convey a very American way of looking at the world. "Whatever you do, give it your best" / "Stand out and you will succeed" / "Follow your heart". But then again, I even found Steve Jobs' commencement speech at Stanford a bit of a cheap marketing trick for a calligraphy class… So in this case, I might have to be the one who needs to review his opinion on the value of these speeches…

115

Moving out time!

This is the time of year when Facebook is flooded with messages such as "Does anyone who is still on campus have an electric screwdriver?" and "Have a closet to give away – ping me if interested." The campus at HBS, which is car-free most of the year, is now flooded with cars and moving trucks picking up the belongings of hundreds of students leaving campus for a next adventure in a different part of town, a different part of the country or a different part of the world. Another common scene on campus is students taking pictures of the iconic buildings they studied and lived in with them and their family. Time to say goodbye to our home of the last two years. Most of us know we will be back one day, be it for a school reunion, a nostalgic visit, or maybe one day to see one's children attend and graduate from the school. So it's not a goodbye – more like a 'see you later?'

PART XV

THE AFTERLIFE

116

The Harvard Alumni Association – online and offline presence

In the weeks prior to graduating from HBS, the usual screen I got after logging in to the HBS website for students had changed. I now had to choose if I wanted to access the MBA Resources (which I had been directed to automatically for the last two years) or if I wanted to access the Alumni Resources. This is when it really struck me that my time at HBS had almost come to an end and that I would soon join the group of now more than 60,000 people who graduated from HBS over the last century.

The online alumni resources provide several interesting tools. Students can find information on alumni activities and events all over the world. They find links to the local alumni organizations in different parts of the world – as I moved to Singapore after school, I got in touch with the Singapore Alumni Club of HBS. And finally, and probably most importantly, students can search HBS's database of HBS alums using different criteria, ranging from name to industry.

I've only used that database once. However, I know of a lot of other HBS students who successfully got in touch with HBS alums in their hunt for jobs or capital for a start-up – both through the database as well as through other routes.

As with most alumni databases, HBS's also struggles to keep the information up-to-date. That's probably why HBS has recently started allowing alums to link their alumni accounts to their LinkedIn profiles, as such ensuring more up-to-date information in the database. However, LinkedIn in general is probably a more updated source of information than the HBS alum database. Though in the end, nothing beats face-to-face contacts or referrals from professors or other HBS people. The online world still has a strong competitor in the offline one – a world that much of the HBS model is based on anyway.

117

HBS donations – philanthropy and/ or personal marketing?!?

In Mid-February of my last academic year at HBS, I received a surprise email with the following subject: "In 100 days…" The email was sent by the "2014 HBS Class Gift Committee". The first part of the mail pointed out that I was indeed only 100 days away from graduation. The rest of the email would relate more to the name of the sender than to the subject, as it informed me of a HBS tradition that was started by the class of 2002. The Class Gift Committee gives graduating students the option to contribute financially to HBS. Students can even choose what they want to donate to – the options include Financial Aid, Educational Innovation, Path-breaking Research or contributing to a global HBS Fund.

As a European, I am less familiar with the concept of "educational philanthropy". Donating to schools is definitely done in Europe, but the number of donors and the dollar values spent are vastly different. A recent article in The Harvard Crimson confirmed some of the crazy amounts of money flowing back to schools. It reported on a $150 million gift to Harvard College by Hedge Fund Manager Kenneth C. Griffin (class of '89) – of which $10 million would flow to the Business School. Comparatively, this amount is not even that excessive. According to the Association to Advance Collegiate Schools of Business (AACSB), there were 52 single gift donations of $1 million or more to business schools in 2013 alone, with 15 of them higher than $10 million. Cornell, Chicago Booth and Stanford GSB top the overall list of highest donations with respective amounts of $350 million, $300 million and $150 million. And according to The Harvard Crimson, the largest donation to a college was a $600 million gift to the California Institute of Technology[189].

Besides these huge gifts, which often end up with someone's name linked to a building or a fellowship, there are also the many small dona-

---

189 http://goo.gl/oMdf5d

tions from across the HBS alumni community. In 2013, HBS collected about $22 million this way. When receiving the Class Gift email, I was surprised to find that I would become part of this donating group even before graduating. When clicking on the link provided in the email, I was redirected to a website to donate. The site adds a competitive aspect to giving money ("Let's beat the class gift record of the class of 2010!"), social pressure ("No need to mark your section, we know who you are and your section will get full credit!") and the final ingredient of giving donors impact on the goal of your contribution ("You get to pick what your gift supports!"). All types of motivators that we discussed during our classes at HBS. At the end of the day, this is a BUSINESS school, right?

In terms of my donation, I started off with a small $50 gift before graduation and increased that amount to $150 the year after graduation[190]. I am still paying off loads of debt related to HBS at the moment, so I don't feel too keen on giving larger amounts of money to the school for now. Another option would be not to give anything at all – I already gave them more than $100,000, right? But then again, it is rumored that not donating to HBS might impact my future offspring's chances of being admitted to HBS. Whether this is true or not, I'll just keep on giving for now. And who knows, maybe one day I'll be in a position to be donating millions of dollars to HBS as well…

118

Now what did I actually learn at HBS?

I have a vivid memory of sitting down at a table on Spangler lawn in Fall. I was having a quick lunch while reading some cases for the next day. I was an RC in my third week or so at HBS and was still trying to keep up with all that was coming at me. I was joined shortly by two girls who came and sat next to me having lunch themselves. We started talking.

---

190 I figured out meanwhile that HBS publishes the names of all donors to the school organized by ranges of the gift (e.g. $0-250, $250-500, etc.) in the HBS alumni magazine. I was happy to notice that my donation matched the donation average…

They were ECs, and they seemed very eager to share some of their experiences and subsequent advice with me. One thing I remember is that they often said something along the lines of "Don't worry, you will learn that here at HBS."

Now that my experience has come to an end, I do wonder however what I actually did learn at HBS. Did I really become a master in finance? Can I solve every supply chain issue in the world? Will I save the corporate life of companies by defining a great strategy for them? That's clearly not how it works. Einstein supposedly said to "not waste your time memorizing things that you could easily look up." In today's Google era, that is a lot of stuff! And the case based MBA is focusing exactly on not remembering stuff, but on how to search for and effectively apply that information.

So the real question is – do I feel I have improved as a professional? And hopefully as a person as well? While impossible to measure in quantitative terms, I do feel HBS has given me a stronger backbone. It has made me aware of my strong points and helped me cope with my weaknesses.

Yet there are some key lessons I recall from my time at HBS – some stuff that just stuck with me or that seemingly has been loaded into my brain in a "The Matrix" style. Find your free 2-year HBS MBA program summarized in a 5 minute read below. Enjoy!

Lesson 1 – Leverage it up baby!

Yep, that's about the one thing I remember from my finance classes. Take on debt, take on more debt and just when you think you got enough, take on some more debt. Make sure your company generates enough cash to pay the interest payments on it – if not, buy some time using Chapter 11 (during which you do not have to pay the interest costs).

Financial analysts consider companies with low levels of debt to be 'poorly managed'. They can be perceived as not trying hard enough to create value for shareholders – a lesson that seems to have been assimilated by a lot of individuals in the U.S. as well, considering the high personal debt levels in that country – not sure that pays off in the same way though.

Lesson 2 – $E(R_i) = R_f + ß_i(E(R_m)-R_f)$

The CAPM model (Capital asset pricing model) – that other thing I should have remembered from my finance classes. THE END.

Lesson 3 – Tesla success story will not last!

Tesla, the world's leading manufacturer of electric cars, has seen an explosion in its sales and its stock price in recent years. As more and more Tesla cars are visible on the road (mostly in rich countries with a focus on environmental issues or with high taxes on emissions), investors were eager to invest in this company. But according to a famous HBS theory, Tesla cars are not disruptive enough to become a long-term success. They don't change the way we drive our cars, they don't improve the use of our cars and they even add limitations to drivers' liberties due to their limited mileage per battery load. Only truly disruptive technologies will succeed – the ones that fundamentally change the way cars are being used.[191] To those that currently hold Tesla stock – time to sell?

Lesson 4 – Empathy is the key to success…

HBS offers a whole range of 'soft' courses on topics such as leadership. Those classes tend to be among my favorites. I was surprised to learn that a recurrent source of long-term success for managers seems to be linked to their level of empathy – it is about fully understanding the drivers and behaviors of your customers/colleagues/superiors/competitors. The real question is – can empathy be developed? And does a HBS MBA contribute to behaving in that way? While it is difficult to tell if I have indeed become a more empathetic leader through my HBS experience, I do believe that studying various leaders and their behaviors has made me a more complete leader – and I hope an improved level of empathy is also one of my newly acquired skills…

Lesson 5 – Loss Aversion

Whenever dealing or negotiating with other people, we should be mindful of how the human brain works. Penalties tend to be more motivating than

---

191 For those interested, find HBS professor Clay Christensen's theories on disruption here: **http://goo.gl/VfvEz1**

rewards. Tons of research demonstrates that the risk of losing something will push people much more than the potential for winning something. Forget about the carrot and go straight to using the stick!

Lesson 6 – Big problems in society are a matter of trade-offs

Other 'soft' courses at HBS tend to focus on macro-economic and societal problems. I was intrigued by the trade-offs that societies have to make between equality and efficiency. As an example, the U.S. has chosen a model that focuses mainly on efficiency. Most European countries have chosen to focus more on equality, losing efficiency in the process. It's an interesting insight when looking at some of the world's biggest problems of today. Which one will you focus on?

Summary

For those that want more than just 6 key lessons on business, you'll just have to apply to HBS! Or alternatively, apply to the newly launched HBX offering, the new online platform for HBS courses. And let me know afterwards if I got the above key lessons right…

119

Do you remember?

This chapter is devoted to HBS students or alumni, as I will list some of the cases that have become classics at HBS or that people might remember for specific reasons. Most of these cases are the ones often referred to in parodies on life at HBS or are the subject of jokes during the HBS show. So, for the HBS crowd, here's me dropping some names for your amusement…

- Heidi Roizen (Heidi Roizen case) and Erik Peterson (Erik Peterson case)
- Compass Box case – everyone loves whisky!
- Tottenham soccer club – Yes, you remember this one because it was hilarious to hear Americans talk about soccer

- Burger King – some people made tons of money!
- Rent-The-Runway – having the 2 founders in class (both former HBS students) was a blast!
- Chateau Margaux – one of the best case protagonists ever to have in class!
- Boston Chicken
- Jan Carlzon (SAS)
- Cialis
- Benihana of Tokyo

120

HBS relics from a HBS relic

Some people throw it all out – I like to keep stuff. Served by the rather large basement at my folks' place, I have been holding on to the most random stuff I put my hands on. While I am far from being a compulsive hoarder, I did collect quite a range of 'random relics' over the years. And when going through some of the HBS stuff I collected during my 2-year MBA, I found some interesting pieces.

First, there is my first ever badge I got at HBS. It dates back to my pre-HBS period – when I was just a working man visiting the HBS campus for fun. I sat in on a class and I was quickly sold by HBS and its teaching model. It was a great experience – one that I would recommend to all students thinking of applying to HBS or other schools. And it turned out to be the first step for me to get a real HBS badge about a year later!

FIELD2 is the amazing program at HBS during which students work as consultants on a project in a developing country. Prior to the trip, students are allowed to state their preferred country to travel to, then an algorithm decides who gets to go where. HBS doesn't simply communicate on the results of the algorithm by email – rather they bring all students together in a room and each group of six gets a box containing pieces of a puzzle. By forming the puzzle (which easily took 15 minutes), we discovered that the puzzle represented a map of Accra, the capital of Ghana. What a great way to discover that we would be spending the first two weeks of January in Ghana for FIELD2! Great job HBS! And yes, the puzzle is safe in my parents' basement now.

Hourly Nerd was a start-up as part of the FIELD3 program at HBS – as part of this program, students receive $5,000 in groups of six to invest in their start-up idea. Most of these start-ups go nowhere, but some hit the jackpot. I found a flyer for Hourly Nerd – it was one of the early marketing initiatives of this young company that is now backed by a couple of million dollars of venture capital. Good luck guys! Find more information on them online.

I already discussed that grades don't matter at HBS, but HBS sure is good at making students believe that grades matter. The tricky thing with getting graded at HBS is that most of it depends on that very subjective thing called class participation. For students' awareness on how they are performing in class, HBS provides a mid-term review for most courses, informing them if they are part of the top 30% of class, the middle 50% or the lagging 20%. I found a review letter from HBS putting me in the top 30% of my operations class! I rule!

Finally, I found a copy of The Harvard Crimson newspaper of my graduation day at HBS. The end of an amazing 2 years at HBS. The end of an era. Bye bye HBS era. Hello HBS relics!

121

Life as an alum – one year out...

It was the large amount of pictures of people wearing graduation gowns that suddenly populated my Facebook timeline that alerted me of the fact that I had been out of school for a year. I figured that it would be interesting to reflect on what happened in my life in the year since receiving my HBS degree.

Changing places... and people...

I still remember my very last day in Cambridge very well. It was June 4th 2014, the eve of my 34th birthday. I remember waking up with a weird feeling that day. I was about to leave a city I had lived in for the last two years. The weather was nice and I decided to go for a last walk in the neighborhood I resided in. I stopped at my favorite local bakery for breakfast and remember taking lots of pictures of streets and buildings that had been a vivid part of my life but that I might not see again for a long time. Yes, I am the nostalgic kind of person...

Later on, I headed back to my Cambridge apartment for the last time. I was alone. My girlfriend that I had been living with throughout my HBS experience had left early that morning on a trip with friends. It was the last time I would ever see her. Just a couple of weeks earlier, we had decided to end our 5-year long relationship. We got engaged only 3 months earlier (in good HBS tradition) but had struggled very hard to keep our relationship alive ever since. I would not only leave a city or an apartment today. I would also leave a partner. All things taken together, I felt I was about to leave a whole life behind.

After my nostalgic neighborhood walk, I started packing my suitcases – all three of them. I was about to embark on a flight late at night back to Belgium. The rest of the day was mostly filled with cleaning up and taking more pictures, this time from inside the apartment. When I pulled shut the door of the apartment behind me for the last time, I felt empty. The one thing that made me feel a bit better that day was that the cute check-in lady of the airline who gave me a huge discount on the charges for my excess luggage. I told her it was my birthday, which she confirmed when looking at my passport – and with some additional smooth small talk from my side she checked in my bags at a third of the normal price. "I still got it," I thought to myself. At least I seemed to have some characteristic traits I could start rebuilding a new life on...

Changing even more places...

I spent the first 60 days after HBS in Europe, spending a lot of time with friends and family. I did some local traveling, had some (HBS) friends visit me in Belgium and started writing the outline of this book. At the end of July, I would move to yet another place – I had accepted a position as a Finance Director in Singapore for a pharmaceuticals company – the same company I had been working for prior to HBS. Singapore is almost literally the opposite place of the world from Boston, is 12 time zones away from it and has temperatures that are at least 40 to 50 degrees Celsius higher than that of Boston in winter! It would be my new home for the next 1 to 2 years.

Changing jobs...

Starting off as the Finance Director for a commercial entity of a multinational pharmaceuticals company in Singapore is not the typical job for a fresh HBS grad – most grads don't chase for finance jobs in corporations and go for either consulting jobs, finance/banking opportunities or more business oriented roles in big corporations. And then there are those who opt for entrepreneurial tracks.

The job is intense but has been a great experience so far. I chose this opportunity as it allowed me to get to know a part of the company I was not very familiar with, because it was a real leadership role within the local entity of Singapore, and because of the international scope of the job (something I had been actively looking for and that was complemented with a nice expat package). But is this the job of my life? Not sure...

At HBS, a lot of focus is channeled toward helping students find that one thing they really enjoy. I have seen people make dramatic career shifts because of that – most of the time for good. Looking back at it, I have not fully optimized my time at HBS in finding my ideal job fit. First of all, do I really know what I want? Will I ever? Second, I am a relatively risk-averse person – hence choosing a stable job in a multinational company above less predictable adventures seemed like a safe option. Third, I feel my current job was a compromise between quality of life, money and adventure. And while it might not be the best fit for me in all three of these aspects, I believe this job might be the best compromise. I don't regret any of it. Close to being one year into the job, I also start reflecting on what's next. And I believe the outcome might just be the result of a new compromise...

Changing more people...

A handful. That would be the answer to the question: "How much of your fellow students have you met up with since leaving HBS?" This is probably not a common representation of most HBS students. My Facebook is full of former students meeting up in the most random places around the world. Whenever they travel, they reach out to fellow students living and working there. It is something I have not been good at doing. I blame my shyness, my introverted personality and also the workload that has come with my job.

I do believe that I might not have fully leveraged on my HBS experience due to my personality and attitude. The HBS network is one of the most valuable assets of my MBA – yet I have been neglecting it for the past year. I have barely reached out to local MBAs here in Singapore. I signed up for a locally organized Alumni event, but had to cancel last minute due to a crisis at work. I was thinking of going to the one year reunion organized by HBS in Boston in May, but quickly figured that the hours of travel (opposite side of the world from Singapore) and the number of days I would have to take off from work during a busy period of the year didn't make sense.

Moreover, I quickly found out that the best place to meet former MBA colleagues are weddings anyway. With all the engagements during the 2-year HBS period, there are quite a lot of weddings going on post-HBS. These can be in India, the U.S., Europe or Singapore for that matter. Some are organized by millionaires, others are the more modest/normal kind. Though what they have in common is that they have a pool of MBAs attending.

Changing temporary places...

As the border security official at Melbourne international airport looks at my passport, I could tell he was annoyed by the poor state it was in. He looked at some of the small rips in one of the papers. He duly inspected some of the creases in my passport cover page. Then he started flipping the pages one by one in search for an empty space to put my first ever Australian stamp in there. I realized then that this passport, which I had received only months before starting my HBS experience, had lived quite the life already. I have always been a traveler of sorts, but HBS definitely left me with a heightened taste for travel and discovery.

During my time at HBS, I travelled to 9 different countries – this might be a low number compared to some other HBS students but quite the average for me (and for most people for that matter)! In the one year I got out of school, I further increased the number of different stamps in my passport with another 12 – helped by the fact that I am living in Asia now (a lot of fresh terrain to cover) and the fact that I am making money again and thus feel much less guilty spending money on plane tickets! I realized that HBS had definitely lowered my threshold for taking planes and planning (quick) trips. I guess this too is part of the transforming leadership experience at HBS…

Changing person?

I get reminded of being a HBS grad through feeds on Facebook from former students, through tons of HBS alum emails and by the reaction of people when I introduce myself to them and tell them I hold an MBA from HBS. But has the MBA impacted my life and my personality as part of the transformational experience they offer (that goes beyond carrying the HBS approval stamp)?

I think I did change, though maybe not in the way I expected to. I learned how to value a company (and have forgotten all about it already). I learned the insights of the energy business, but work in pharmaceuticals. I learned how to think about things in a different way, and try to apply this as much as possible in my current life.

I also learned to accept myself the way I am – with all my faults. I learned that I have to stop adapting myself to others – I have to follow my own thoughts and pursue my personal ambitions. I learned that I have brilliant moments that I alternate with moments of stupidity. I learned to admire some people that are very different from me but have so much to offer. Finally, after spending 2 months there for my summer internship, I learned that I love Japan.

To me, life is all about learning, and HBS was a part of that. I believe it is too early to tell if it was a truly transformational experience. And maybe I am not the best person to refer to for this, as I might not have truly opened myself to the power of the HBS transformation.

Would I recommend HBS to others? Definitely! We only live once, and HBS is a great experience to have in our one precious life. Is it for everyone? No, definitely not. It is intense, expensive and very business focused. It is a part of my life that I really enjoyed. And now, to use the words of one of my professors at HBS, I just need to make sure that HBS was not the peak in my life...

To be continued...

PART

XVI

SAYING THANKS...

I mentioned the Saying Thanks initiative launched by my class of 2014 at HBS earlier in this book. As part of this initiative, students thank both the academic and the support staff at HBS for all the great work done. Yet, I want to thank those people once more in this book.

Thanks to those working in Spangler Cafeteria for all the good food and great service. Thanks to those wiping the boards after class. Thanks to those keeping all HBS facilities clean and keeping the streets free of snow in winter and the grass nice and tidy in summer. Thanks to the hidden HBS talents – the case writers, the support staff, people working for career services. Thanks to those working for admissions at HBS for letting me in. Thanks to my fellow HBS colleagues. Thanks to all the other ones I forget to mention but were part of my great experience at HBS.

Special thanks to my former girlfriend Sara Hess for continuously pushing me to apply to HBS, to advise me to start the blog HBSTimes.com and to stimulate me to write this book. Special thanks also to some of the people who helped me to review my application to HBS. Thanks to my recommenders for believing in me, for supporting me throughout my career and for taking the time to write a review on me – Benoît, Nathalie and Paul. Thanks to the BAEF – the Belgian American Educational Fund – for providing me with an interest-free loan to help me pay for this endeavor. Thanks to my employer for sponsoring part of the cost of the MBA as well. And, finally, I would like to kiss the nose of an INSEAD grad who is not only special to me, but also did a fantastic job motivating me through the painstaking task of finishing this book.

Thanks to family and friends for providing support and guidance when I needed it the most. Thanks for staying closely in touch with me despite my many international endeavors. I couldn't be more fortunate to have all of you so close to me despite the often important geographical distances.

PART

XVII

ADDITIONAL
DOCUMENTS

122

Useful websites and services

Some websites to check out if interested in applying to HBS or other business schools:

Beat the GMAT	**http://goo.gl/NuRZWd**
GMAT Tutor	**http://goo.gl/yxaJKu**
(previously known as masterthegmat.com)	
POETS&Quants	**http://goo.gl/UTLeaI**
My Blog HBSTimes!	**http://goo.gl/Opm1QS**
A video on the case method at HBS:	**http://goo.gl/kSCGY9**

a

b

c

d

e

123

My HBS application test scores

For those interested, here were my test scores:

TOEFL: Test Date: June 10th 2011

Reading:	29
Listening:	30
Speaking:	29
Writing:	25
Total:	113

GMAT: Test Date: August 22nd 2011

Verbal:	44	(percentile 97)
Quant:	47	(percentile 76)
Total:	730	(percentile 96)
AWA:	4.0	

124

The essays that got me into HBS[192]

1. Tell us about three of your accomplishments. (600 words)

A couple of years ago, while working in the global finance department at ABC I was approached to manage a project aimed at creating a 10-year outlook on the firm's gross profit margin. I baptized the project 'Bambi,' Biologicals Allocation Model for Business Improvement. Bambi taught me two important lessons. First of all, never name a project after a famous Walt Disney character—it will hunt you for years. Second, the project made me aware of my talent and passion for strategic corporate finance and its accompanying decision making process.

---

192   Please note I did change names of people and companies for privacy reasons

For Bambi, I met with dozens of the most influential professionals within the ABC manufacturing organization. I spent hours reviewing inconsistencies between business cases made in the years prior to the project, aligning capital expenditure plans and evaluating long term contract deals. I was skeptical about qualitative inputs and hungry for data, which was very dispersed within the organization. I dug deep for numbers. I ultimately used my findings to design and program a model that simulated the impact of strategic decisions on the gross profit margin. Bambi was recently used to assess the potential outcome of an investment worth xxxm£ and is a source of reference for the company's long-term ambitions. I am proud to have made such a strong contribution to the firm and have also enjoyed reaping the benefits of greater visibility within the company as I now am considered an expert in strategic planning.

I love working with data; but I also love working with people. During my time as a consultant I often enjoyed participating in evening happy hours and other social events. I found these informal opportunities to interact with colleagues a great opportunity to learn more about clients and build relationships across departments. Coming to ABC, I quickly realized that the company's rapid growth had created a fragmented organization. People worked in their own silos. This sometimes led to inefficiencies when different departments failed to communicate with one another as part of the problem-solving process.

In 2008, I brought together five talented young professionals to help me solve this problem. Our idea was to schedule a social gathering where each of us would invite two or three motivated young colleagues to attend. The first event was a huge success. Later on, similar events were organized and ABCNet eventually expanded to include more than 50 people. At an ABCNet event people from all over the company, who would likely never have met otherwise, talk with one another, exchanging experiences and ideas. I believe it's always easier to ask someone you know for help and to this end ABCNet has proven to be an effective tool for facilitating communication across departments at ABC.

Finally, outside of work I'm a music-o-holic that long dreamed of learning to play an instrument. My ultimate stroke of inspiration came while studying in Madrid, Spain. Every day on my commute I passed a very talented guitar player who performed in the subway. His music and clever way of entertaining, complete with a small sign next to his tip jar that read "for my Ferrari," inspired me to finally give my musical ambitions a chance. I bought a cheap guitar and spent hours in my room trying to figure out the chords of my favorite songs. Over the years I've become quite a good musician, added the electric guitar and ukulele to my repertoire, and even formed a band with some friends. This experience has provided me with endless hours of entertainment and has also shown me the value of exploring my diverse interests.

2. Tell us three setbacks you have faced. (600 words)

My first important professional setback came shortly after starting at ABC. In my new role, I was responsible for tracking performance of the global operations management team—a difficult task. At that time, ABC had no standardized metrics for evaluating operational performance; rather each production site utilized its own method leaving no standard of comparison.

My solution was to create a set of performance indicators that were concise, standardized, and aligned with senior management's priorities. After receiving the approval of my managers, I set out to advertise my great new evaluation method to ABC's production site leaders. To my surprise, the site directors disapproved of my proposal, instead praising the benefits of the old system. Lack of approval from the site directors ultimately slowed implementation and forced my superiors and I to back down on some of my recommended changes. Later I understood the source of the site directors' disapproval. Many felt threatened by the new method as it would allow for a comparison of performance across sites. This was precisely my aim though I had failed to see how the site directors themselves would respond to this change.

Watching my idea slowed and altered by inter-office dynamics taught me to more thoroughly consider the political aspects of innovation. Now when implementing major changes I make communicating with my stakeholders a priority so as to avoid problems later on.

Outside of work I'm a soccer enthusiast who a couple of years ago started a local soccer club with some friends. Our team, the "Swotters," participated in weekly games with a league outside of Brussels. One night, after a seemingly innocent contact with another player, I felt intense pain in my knee. A trip to the doctor revealed the cartilage was severely damaged requiring surgery. Post-operative, it took me six months to walk normally again. Although I can now do other sports, my soccer days are over. After the incident, I still wanted to remain part of the Swotters so I took a seat on the bench and became the Swotters' biggest fan. The bench, I found, offered me a new perspective on the game. I began to notice tendencies in the team's play and used my observations to offer advice. Before long, I was promoted to coach. In this role, I implemented a few small but instrumental changes. As the end of the season drew near I was proud to watch the normally average Swotters win the provincial cup. The Swotters' trophy remains a symbol to me of the importance of teamwork and flexibility in changing conditions.

Another setback comes from an early attempt at entrepreneurship. While still a student some of my fellow classmates and I decided to launch a dot com company. We created a website, Indigo, focused on connecting young graduates with companies. In no time, we collected 250 resumes in our database, signed two important sponsor deals and were just inches away from signing a collaboration deal with XYZ, a leader in European online job portals. Then everything changed.

The famous dotcom bubble burst of early 2002 annihilated our customer base and sponsorship deals. XYZ lost all interest. As our dreams of entrepreneurial success crumbled, we sold Indigo to a competitor, barely breaking even. My dreams of entering the working world as an entrepreneur were brought to an abrupt end. Reflecting on the decision to sell, I believe we responded too emotionally to our first major setback. In future entrepreneurial endeavors, I will strive to think through my options more clearly and avoid acting out of fear.

3. Why do you want an MBA? (400 words)

I've been passionate about business since I was a little boy watching my father, a renowned Belgian pastry chef and entrepreneur, grow his business from the ground up. Over the years I have pursued my interest in business through my studies, several years of consulting, and a longer term commitment to ABC. These experiences have allowed me to acquire a unique skill set in finance and operations management as well as strong leadership capabilities.

Reflecting on my work experiences to date, the projects I've most enjoyed are those which allowed me to exercise a greater degree of entrepreneurship. This observation harkens back to my early exposure to entrepreneurship in my father's business and reminds me of my ultimate goal—to start my own business. In the short term, I would like to pursue some of the areas I am most passionate about, such as global healthcare and innovation management. An MBA would allow me to accomplish this goal through classes, internships, and additional professional experiences after graduation. Five years from now, I want the sum of these experiences to result in my own start-up. I believe the MBA program at HBS presents me with unprecedented opportunities to pursue my goals. In conversation with Professor DEF I learned of various initiatives to support entrepreneurship such as the Business Plan Contest and Entrepreneurship Club. HBS alumni have directed me to explore the new Harvard Innovation Lab where I could develop and hone my business ideas through interactions with students from across the university.

While visiting HBS, I discovered the MBA classroom itself to be a unique breeding ground for entrepreneurial ideas. I found the conversations sparked by the case method inspiring and would revel in the opportunity to make these classes part of my daily routine. Further, I want any business I create to be a global one. To accomplish this task I need a global network expanding outside of my European borders. HBS will provide me with a once in a lifetime opportunity to grow a large and influential network in a short amount of time. For me, an MBA is a chance to explore my interests more broadly, interact with students from around the world, and pursue my passion for entrepreneurship in an environment that supports such endeavors. I have done my research and I am confident that HBS has what I am looking for.

4. Describe a time when you had to make a difficult decision. (400 words)

I was 20 years old when my Dad came to me and offered his life's work—a pastry shop that in just over 20 years had grown into an establishment respected nationwide for its fine desserts. As my father's oldest son, I knew the day would come when we would discuss his succession. However, I had never expected it to come so quickly. My father was 49-years old and in good shape. Still today, I cannot understand his motivation to suddenly bow out of such a successful career. But speaking to him at the time, I knew his decision was final.

Growing up, the family-business played an important role in my life. I remember helping my dad make chocolates at a young age. Later on, I supported some of the general management activities of the 40-employee business. I enjoyed growing up in this environment, and I believe it instilled in me certain values—hard-working, resilient, and entrepreneurial. When my father came to me with the question of taking over I was just about to finalize my undergraduate studies and begin my masters. I had been drafting a personal vision of my goals, aimed at starting off in a corporate career with the long-term ambition of starting my own business. I reasoned that a commitment to run the family business would have tremendous consequences. I would likely have to drop out of school and leave my goals behind. I was forced to choose between following my own plans or sustaining my father's life's work. It was a very difficult decision but I ultimately told my Dad I wasn't interested.

My Dad sold the shop in early 2001, just a couple of months after our first talk. Unfortunately, the buyers were poor businessmen and managed to bankrupt a successful business in only a couple of years. It was an emotionally profound experience for my family, as we saw a great business fall into decline and a lot of people that used to work for us lose their jobs. If I could go back in time, I would still decide to continue with my studies. However, I think I would suggest alternatives to my Dad's proposal such as allowing the family to maintain majority ownership of the business until I felt more prepared to decide. Overall, I am satisfied with my decision and remain determined to pursue my goals.

18077961R00151

Printed in Great Britain
by Amazon